The
Divine
Virginia

Virginia Zucchi at the age of twenty-four. A portrait photograph taken in Rome in 1873. *(Museo alla Scala, Milan)*

The Divine Virginia

A Biography of Virginia Zucchi

Ivor Guest

MARCEL DEKKER, INC.   New York and Basel

PROVENANCE OF THE ILLUSTRATIONS

Ashmolean Museum, Oxford
Bakhrushin Theatre Museum, Moscow
Biblioteca Braidense, Milan
British Library, London
Dance Collection, Museum of Performing Arts, New York
Harvard Theatre Collection, Cambridge, Massachusetts
Musée de l'Opéra, Paris
Museo alla Scala, Milan
Museo de Storia ed Arte, Trieste
Soviet Archives
Victoria and Albert Museum, London
Courtesy of Mrs. Carla Hackett Quijano
Collection of Natalia Roslavleva

MARCEL DEKKER, INC.

270 Madison Avenue, New York, New York 10016

LIBRARY OF CONGRESS CATALOG CARD NUMBER: 76-20006

ISBN: 0-8247-6492-7

Current printing (last digit):
10 9 8 7 6 5 4 3 2 1

PRINTED IN THE UNITED STATES OF AMERICA

For
Helen Willard,
a true friend of all scholars
dedicated to theatre research,
with affection.

Preface

In the last three decades of the nineteenth century ballet seemed
to have lost its appeal. Its decline had been surprisingly rapid. For,
only a generation or two earlier, through the creative genius of
choreographers such as Filippo Taglioni and Perrot, and the
magic of Marie Taglioni and the pleiad of ballerinas who followed
her, ballet had been identified with the Romantic movement and
had known a period of unparalleled brilliance. Since then new
trends had followed those of Romanticism in literature, painting,
music and other arts; but ballet had remained untouched by such
influences, had lost its vitality and had sunk to the level of a
minor form of entertainment.

In London it had even lost its place in the opera house
and taken root in the brash surroundings of the music hall. In
Paris it had managed to retain its foothold at the Opéra, but had
become so effete that it was no longer considered as a serious
theatrical art. In Italy the decadence of choreographic taste was
all too evident in the extravaganzas of Manzotti—*Excelsior* and
Amor—and it needed no particular insight to see that ballet
totally lacked the creative impulse that was then motivating the
development of opera in the later period of Giuseppe Verdi.

In Russia, whence the renaissance of ballet was eventually
to come, conditions were somewhat better. Unlimited support
from the Tsar's privy purse gave St. Petersburg an advantage that
was denied to London, Paris and the cities of Italy. But even
there the popularity of ballet was on the wane in the 1870s, and
the revival that took place in the succeeding decades was due

not to any significant development in choreographic art, for the
ballet establishment was unshakably conservative, but to the
sensational impact made upon the Russian public by a succession
of brilliant Italian dancers.

For the most part they were distinguished by an unprecedented virtuosity, which in time Russian dancers would succeed
in emulating—Legnani's thirty-two *fouettés* remain in *Swan Lake*
as a memorial to these technicians—but the first, the most
celebrated and the most significant of them all, Virginia Zucchi,
was of a very different calibre. She was an artist of the theatre
in the most complete sense, a dancer who interpreted her roles
with such a range of feeling and such understanding of character
as to command comparison with the other great dancer-actress
of her century, Fanny Elssler, and—a rare phenomenon in those
days of balletic decadence—to be spoken of in the same breath
with the greatest figures of the dramatic stage.

The legacy of Virginia Zucchi was a significant factor in
the revival of ballet in the early twentieth century. To many
Russian dancers she had become, in a sense, a legend, while
several men who were to be counted among Diaghilev's closest
associates had seen her in their youth and been fired with an
unquenchable passion for the ballet. One has only to read
Alexandre Benois' vivid memories of her to realize how powerful
was her inspiration and to be set wondering what course ballet
might have taken had she not awakened his interest at this
impressionable stage in his life. And the discovery that so many
of his contemporaries also recognised her as a formative influence
leaves one in no doubt as to her significance in the development
of ballet, not merely as an artist of exceptional talent, but as a
truly inspirational force.

Unlike other great figures in the history of ballet—for
example, Noverre, Taglioni, Fokine, Nijinsky, Pavlova, whose
contributions were fully recognised during their careers—Virginia

Zucchi could have sensed only vaguely the extent of her influence. And indeed, even now, nearly fifty years after her death, her career, apart from her seasons in Russia, is virtually unrecorded. The purpose of these pages, therefore, is to remedy a long-standing neglect and redress an injustice and to set down, in the modest measure that is unavoidable at this distance of time, the achievements of a dancer-actress who was without a peer in her time and who fired the imagination of a generation that was to raise ballet to the maturity it enjoys today.

Holland Park, London   Ivor Guest

Acknowledgments

It was my friend, G. B. L. Wilson, who first awakened my
interest in Virginia Zucchi when he casually remarked one day
that there seemed to be a dearth of photographs of her in his
vast library of books on ballet. Having now come to the end of
my biographical quest, I hope I have satisfied his curiosity about
a truly great figure in the history of ballet who, as his remark
implied, had been most unjustly neglected. With his unfailing
good will, he has, once again, allowed me to bully him into
reading my work in typescript, and thus I have a double indebtedness to him to acknowledge.

Much of the material on Virginia Zucchi's career had to
be laboriously unearthed from libraries and archives where, as
always, I have received the utmost courtesy and assistance: in
Italy, the Biblioteca Braidense and the Museo alla Scala of Milan
and the Museo di Storia ed Arte of Trieste; in Paris, the Musée et
Bibliothèque de l'Opéra, the Bibliothèque de l'Arsenal and the
Bibliothèque de l'Institut des Langues et Civilisations Orientales;
in London, the British Library, the Victoria and Albert Museum
and the British Theatre Museum; in Oxford, the Ashmolean
Museum; in the U.S.S.R., the Soviet Archives and the Bakhrushin
Museum, Moscow; and in the U.S.A., the Dance Collection of The
New York Public Library at Lincoln Center, Astor, Lenox and
Tilden Collections, and the Harvard Theatre Collection.

To many of my fellow theatre historians and specialists
I have increased my debts of gratitude for generous assistance
that have accumulated over many years: Vera Krasovskaya,

Natalia Roslavleva and Yuri Slonimsky in the U.S.S.R., Helen Willard, Genevieve Oswald and Walter Terry in the U.S.A., Friderica Derra de Moroda in Austria, Marie-Françoise Christout in France, Janina Pudełek in Poland, and Kurt Petermann in the German Democratic Republic. To my sorrow three very eminent dance historians who not only gave practical help, but encouraged and inspired me in my work—Lillian Moore, Walter Toscanini and Yuri Bakhrushin—have not survived to see this book in print.

    I am also most grateful to several members of Virginia Zucchi's family for their help in providing information, particularly about her later years, and supplying photographs: her niece, the late Mrs. Virginia Zucchi Hackett; her great-niece, Mrs. Carla Hackett Quijano; and her great-grandson, Charles G. Braun. My thanks are also due to the late Carlotta Zambelli and to Vincenzo Celli for sharing their memories of Virginia Zucchi with me. For permission to quote from important authorities I am indebted to Arnold Haskell, for extracts from his *Diaghileff*, *Balletomania* and *Ballet Panorama*; Editions Albin Michel, for extracts from *Retour au Palais Farnèse*; Hutchinson Publishing Group Ltd. for extracts from Olga Racster's *Master of the Russian Ballet*; Putnam & Co., for extracts from Alexandre Benois' *Reminiscences of the Russian Ballet*; Chatto & Windus, for extracts from Alexandre Benois' *Memoirs*; Garnstone Press for extracts from Constantin Stanislavsky's *My Life in Art*; Victor Gollancz Ltd. for extracts from the memoirs of Kshesinskaya, *Dancing in Petersburg*; and George Allen & Unwin for extracts from Peter Lieven's *Birth of Ballets Russes.* My thanks are also due to all those libraries, museums and private collectors who have allowed me to illustrate this book from items in their collections: the provenance of the pictures reproduced is specified beneath each illustration. I have to record my gratitude to Mrs. John Willcocks and J. Stewart Barker for help in translating, to Lisa Finzi for doing research for me in Milan, and to my secretary, Sandy Mitchell.

Finally, my wife has not only read the work at the various stages of its gestation and given me invaluable advice and encouragement, but cheerfully accepted yet another spectral rival in our family circle!

Holland Park, London   Ivor Guest

Contents

Illustrations

OTHER WORKS BY THE AUTHOR

Napoleon III in England
The Ballet of the Second Empire
The Romantic Ballet in England
Fanny Cerrito
Victorian Ballet Girl
Adeline Genée
The Alhambra Ballet
The Dancer's Heritage
La Fille Mal Gardée (ed.)
The Empire Ballet
A Gallery of Romantic Ballet
The Romantic Ballet in Paris
Dandies and Dancers
Carlotta Zambelli
Two Coppélias
Fanny Elssler
Pas de Quatre
Le Ballet de l'Opéra

A Miracle Indeed!

"Zucchi was a genius, so vital and stimulating that no one could remain indifferent to her influence . . . . Her example proved that the dancer as an artist could be the equal of a Sarah Bernhardt or a Duse."[1]

These words of Walter Nouvel, the friend and counsellor of Diaghilev, cast a revealing light on the astonishing power of Virginia Zucchi as a performer and the inspiration with which she enriched the art of theatrical dancing. Only a rare genius could have burst into the history of ballet with such dazzling brilliance to occupy, alone, a lofty peak above even her most eminent contemporaries. That her career coincided with a period generally recognized as one of decadence only underlines the extraordinary nature of her gift. The word genius defies precise definition, but it has been said that talent is that which is in a man's power, and genius that in whose power a man is. It is by that measure that the full meaning of the appellation bestowed on Zucchi at the height of her career—the Divine Virginia—can best be appreciated.

Unlike the genius of a poet or a composer, which can be preserved for all time, that of a theatrical artist before the days of recording techniques could not survive the moment of performance except in the tenuous strands of human memory. That Zucchi possessed a quality that was both extraordinary and personal to herself is clearly evident from the descriptions of those who saw her dance and act and from the inspiration she gave to younger dancers who observed her artistry at first hand.

1

Her life spanned two of the greatest periods in the history of ballet. She was born when Fanny Elssler and Fanny Cerrito, two of the greatest stars of the Romantic ballet, were still dancing, and she died a year after the Diaghilev Ballet had run its full course. When she was beginning her career, the golden age of Romantic ballet lay in the recent past, but some of the mystery and vitality that had enhanced the performances of that time had vanished. The style of the established ballerinas of the early eighteen-sixties—Caterina Beretta, Carolina Pochini, Amina Boschetti, Amalia Ferraris—seemed to belong to an earlier age, and for all its correctness their dancing appeared, to younger eyes, academic and somewhat arid. Virginia Zucchi was not built to personify the spiritual creatures who obsessed the imaginations of choreographers. By the accepted standards of the time her figure was too full and her allure too openly inviting. But for the younger generation she represented a new type of ballerina. She was, as her contemporary Francesco Giarelli perceived, "the precursor of a new school. She was the Emile Zola of the ballet. She was born in order to revive the anaemic and languorous [Marguerite] Gautier* with warm and plentiful new blood. Once launched on her career, Zucchi advanced triumphantly to attack and conquer the senses. Not for nothing did she recall the dance styles of Cerrito and Elssler. The nymph of the ancient choreographic Olympus was banished and replaced by the daughter of Maenad consumed with the frenzy of Bacchus."[2]

Virginia Zucchi's career as a dancer, from 1864 to 1898, was passed mainly in her native Italy and in Russia. In Italy, with its multiplicity of theatres offering many more opportunities than dancers enjoyed elsewhere, she acquired her vast stage experience. But it was in Russia that she fulfilled herself most completely and there that her influence was most strongly felt.

*The consumptive heroine of Alexandre Dumas fils' novel, *La Dame aux camélias.*

When she arrived in St. Petersburg in 1885, with the summer of her youth already behind her, ballet aroused little enthusiasm and performances were thinly attended. Virtually single-handed and almost overnight she reversed this situation, and by the time she paid her last visit to Russia seven years later, the golden age of the Imperial ballet had dawned. The lessons of Zucchi and the Italian ballerinas who came to Russia in her wake had been quickly learnt. Already a new generation of Russian ballerinas was emerging, headed by Matilda Kshesinskaya and Olga Preobrazhenskaya, who could hold their own against any international celebrity imported from abroad, and in the St. Petersburg Theatre School an unprecedented array of talent was being formed. The ground was being prepared for the momentous revelation of Russian ballet that Diaghilev was soon to unveil. To this artistic revolution Zucchi was to make a contribution of great significance, as Arnold Haskell quickly perceived in his conversations with many of the protagonists of the Diaghilev Ballet. "By directly inspiring Kshesinskaya, and by moving Volkonsky, Benois, Nouvel and others, it may have been she, more than any other single artist, who saved ballet, and gave to it its new importance," he wrote in his biography of Diaghilev. "And thus it is that the great dancer survives, if not always in memory, yet in actual concrete service to her art, long after she has ceased to dance and to live."[3]

Indeed, if it had not been for Zucchi, Kshesinskaya, the first Russian to receive the title of *prima ballerina assoluta*, might have abandoned the stage as a child. When she first saw Zucchi on the Imperial stage she was a fourteen-year-old pupil at the Theatre School. She recalled in her memoirs: "I was already receiving small roles which I strove to interpret to the best of my powers and which even won me praises. But I had no faith in what was being done in our company, and my dancing yielded me no deep satisfaction. I was seized with doubts: had I chosen the career which suited me? I cannot imagine where all that might have led me had it not been for the arrival of Virginia Zucchi, who imme-

diately and radically, altered my state of mind, revealing to me the
true meaning of our art. . . . I felt an overwhelming, unforgettable
sensation when I watched her. . . . She gave all the movements of
classical ballet extraordinary charm and astonishing beauty of expression. . . . Her acting henceforth became true art for me, and I
understood that the essence of such art does not lie exclusively in
virtuosity and technique. I realised that technique, far from being
an end, is only a means."[4]

To Kshesinskaya Zucchi's art seemed timeless. Thinking
back, in her later years, to the great personalities of the ballet she
had known in her youth, she realised that some would not match
up to the standards of a later age because of developments in technique and changes in taste. But Zucchi, she was sure, would appeal
to a twentieth-century audience with the same eloquent power and
immediacy that thrilled the public of the 1880s.

Tamara Karsavina was too young to have seen Zucchi dance,
for she was born in the same year that the Divine Virginia first
came to Petersburg. But when she entered the Theatre School,
Zucchi had virtually become a legend and details of her technique
and interpretation had already become part of the fabric of
Russian ballet tradition. Her renderings of some of the great roles
of the repertory—Lise in *La Fille mal gardée,* Esmeralda, and the
mimed part of Fenella in the opera *La Muette de Portici*—were
accepted models. And from the classroom Karsavina remembered
a certain combination of steps for developing a closely adhering
high *retiré* that was known as the "*pas de Zucchi*" because Zucchi
had enriched it with such original and beautiful movements of the
arms.

The distinctive quality of this *enchaînement* lay in the expressiveness of the movements, and it was here that Zucchi was
unique. In many histories of ballet she is named as the first of a
long line of Italian ballerinas who dazzled St. Petersburg with their
technical virtuosity. Indeed, she did not lack the brilliant technique
of the Italian school of her time, but many of her compatriots—

Antonietta Dell'Era, for example, and Giovannina Limido, who was perhaps the most remarkable of them all—excelled her in sheer virtuosity. The true secret of her greatness lay in another direction, in "her marvellous mimicry, her hypnotic acting."[5] While the other Italians stretched the purely technical possibilities of the dance, her contribution was more subtle and more profound. In the words of Valerian Svetlov, "she revealed that the ballet is not merely dancing, but drama too; a drama that is dumb and all the more expressive. It is obviously much more difficult to convey a dramatic situation, a psychological emotion, a stirring of the soul by an expression of the body and the play of the features alone than to move the audience with a ringing tirade in verse or prose. Those who saw Zucchi dance will never forget her tragic Esmeralda, nor her joyful, mischievous Swanilda in *Coppélia*. From that time on a dramatic element entered the classical dance and began to play a very large part in Russian ballet."[6] This was, of course, an over-simplification, but Zucchi did indeed, as Svetlov wrote elsewhere, "renew the tie between the dance and the plastic drama, thereby leading it back to its first source in antiquity."[7]

It was significant that, when critics related her to other eminent figures in the history of the stage, it was to actresses rather than to ballerinas that their thoughts turned, to Rachel, Ristori, Sarah Bernhardt and Duse; and that, when a dancer was taken as a point of reference, it was the dramatic Fanny Elssler rather than the spiritual Taglioni who came to mind. The caricaturist Teja acknowledged this when he depicted Zucchi as Hamlet, in company with the great actor Ernesto Rossi in travesty as a ballerina, and a later writer suggested that if she had been born half a century later she might have become a star of the silent cinema.

There was an element of truth in this surmise, for—like the great actresses with whom she was compared, and in common, too, with Greta Garbo and the great mimetic stars of the early cinema—Virginia Zucchi was one of those very rare and original artists, *monstres sacrés* as the French call them, who do not fit into the conventional pattern of their art but mould their art to the contours of their genius. In her case her genius was so personal to herself that it survived, not through imitators of her technique and method, but in the new possibilities which she revealed in the area of interpretation. This inspiration nurtured not only the remarkable younger generation of Russian dancers that followed her but also teachers and choreographers. The dance historian, Alexandre Pleshcheyev, declared that Marius Petipa's artistic and aesthetic taste was undeniably influenced to advantage by Zucchi's performances. And Pavel Gerdt, who taught for many years at the Petersburg Theatre School and counted Pavlova, Fokine, Karsavina and Vaganova among his pupils, was so overwhelmed by the aesthetic expressiveness of Zucchi's acting that he enriched and expanded his method with many touches he had learnt from his firsthand observations of her art.

The dramatic strength and the bold realism which Zucchi brought to her interpretations, to a degree not previously attained, made an immediate impact not only on her fellow dancers but, with equally far-reaching effect, on the public. The youth of the time, for whom the ballet had held little appeal before her arrival, were overwhelmed. Many of them acquired, through her, a life-long love of the dance, and among their number were men who were to play a leading role in the great development that would profoundly transform the aesthetics of ballet in the early twentieth century.

One of these was Prince Serge Volkonsky, who during his brief term as Director of the Imperial Theatres from 1899 to 1901 endeavoured against great odds to introduce reforms. As a youth he had been a keen follower of the drama, but ballet seemed an illogical and affected spectacle. Then, in 1885, he saw Zucchi dancing in the pleasure garden of Kin Grust and, in his own words, "I realised that ballet dancing could have a 'meaning.' She was one of the greatest mimes I have ever seen. Everything about her seemed

to speak—eyes, shoulders, hands and fingers. I shall never forget her
lovely expressive back, when she turned it to the public. . . . [In
Brahma] she had to conquer music, story and decor, and the
mood of an audience who had come to see—not art, but physical
prowess and tricks! What was important was the fact that her
movements, in their preparation and in their climax, fell in time
with the music. That may seem obvious to you now, but in those
days music and movement were very far apart. This, then, became
for me the main exigency to which mime in dancing must respond,
and it was the main exigency just because at that time it was the
most neglected one. Little by little through my interest in the
mime I was won over to see what vast possibilities lay in ballet
and began to interest myself in the purely dramatic side."[8] This
spark that Zucchi ignited was to lead Volkonsky into realms beyond the confines of classical ballet—to Delsarte and his theories
of expressive gesture, and to Dalcroze and his system of eurhyth-
mics.

Even more momentous in its consequences was the impact
she made on the youthful Alexandre Benois, who, like Volkonsky,
was converted to the dance as he sat in the wooden theatre at Kin
Grust. If it had not been for the revelation that came to him on
that summer evening, he might never have become such a devotee
of the ballet, and without his enthusiasm the talents of his friend
Diaghilev might well have been channeled in another direction
with consequences that one hardly dares to imagine. In all justice,
therefore, Benois should be allowed the last word on the essence
of Zucchi's art. "She was not a Sylphide," he explained in his
memoirs, "but when the scene demanded the impersonation of a
real woman with purely feminine charm, then Virginia was incomparable and convincing. It was impossible not to believe that she
experienced all the emotions she expressed to the full not only with
the mime of her beautiful yet sweet and significant face, but with
all the movements of her body, now impetuous, now soft and infi-

nitely tender. . . . I knew people who were moved to tears at
Zucchi's performances, not because the dramatic situation in the
ballet was so moving, but because it was so beautiful. This was art
in which there was not a breath of artificiality. A miracle indeed!"[9]

A Local Reputation in the Making

It was a troubled world into which Virginia Zucchi was born, in the small city of Parma, at half-past eight in the morning of February 10th, 1849. The Italian peninsula was in turmoil. The struggle to cast off the yoke of the Austrian Empire and create a united Italy had erupted violently the year before, and the people of Parma had played their part bravely by expelling their duke and voting for union with Piedmont. Since then the Austrians had recovered somewhat from their early setbacks, but the issue was by no means settled. In fact, another round of the struggle had opened the very day before Virginia's birth, when Manin's short-lived Roman republic had been proclaimed. For Italians these were stirring and romantic times, and as the child grew up she must have identified herself with the hopes and disappointments and, ultimately, the triumph of the Risorgimento, the movement of national revival. All this inevitably marked her as a fervent patriot. To the end of her days she was to remain passionately Italian, and it is not surprising that her art was essentially a product of the Italian theatre—her dancing unmistakably imprinted with the style of the Italian school and her miming fundamentally the expression of Italian temperament.

Her birthplace was a modest apartment in the centre of the town, at No. 6 Borgo Paggeria, conveniently close to the Treasury, where her father Vicenzo worked as a halberdier. To help with the family finances his wife Maria, whose maiden name was Gerbella, had been teaching at a local school, but she gave up this employment when she started her family. Virginia was their first-born.

9

In 1850 another daughter, Costantina, was born, and later the
family was increased by the arrival of two sons, Achille in 1854
and Vittorio in 1859. The humble station of the Zucchis can perhaps be judged from the occupations of the witnesses who accompanied Vicenzo when he registered the births of his offspring—a
messenger and a clerk, a process server, a door-keeper and a
cleaner.

Their eldest child was launched into the world with the
names Virginia Eurosia Teresa. Most of her early education was received at home, no doubt from her mother; but the absence of normal schooling did not set her back, for not only was her mother a
practised teacher, but Virginia herself was quick-witted and naturally intelligent, and eager to learn. She was also an unusual child,
as her father discovered quite early when he saw her leaning out of
a window and miming some experience to a young friend across
the street. Like most little girls Virginia took dancing lessons; she
excelled in the school shows, and danced waltzes and polkas so
beautifully that kind friends often suggested she was good enough
for the stage. Nobody took this advice very seriously until the
Sfornis, a prominent family in Parma, brought a more powerful
influence to bear. Signora Sforni praised the child's talent so per-
suasively to her husband that he offered to bear the expense of
taking her to Milan to train under the best teachers available. At
first Virginia's mother refused even to consider such an idea, but
eventually she was won over, the necessary arrangements were
made, and the whole family uprooted themselves from Parma and
moved to Milan.

On their arrival there they lost no time in making themselves known to Augusto Hus, who directed the School of Ballet
attached to the opera house of La Scala. Hus was not prepared to
enroll Virginia in the school, but he did arrange for her to study
privately under his assistant, Pasquale Corbetta. This was not
such a favour as it appeared, for Corbetta was a very uninspiring
teacher. In time Virginia realised this, and she once became so

exasperated that she threw up her arms in despair and exclaimed: "Of course I shall end up among the hens."[1] It was clearly time to move on, and she left Corbetta to study with other teachers, including Giuseppe Ramaccini and Lodovico Montani.

She received an unusual and varied training, very different from what the Scala School would have provided. Indeed it may well have been to her advantage that she was not admitted there, although at the time it was such a blow to her pride that she used to walk in and out of the School entrance so that her friends might think she studied there. In later years critics and connoisseurs were to puzzle over her artistic ancestry, and perhaps the most accurate conclusion was expressed in these words by a writer who knew her: "She was her own pupil, I would say, and I think this is the truth. She studied a little with one teacher, a little with another, but no one person can boast of having made her what she is."[2] Whatever the influences that formed her as a dancer, the results of her training were beyond doubt. She proved a model pupil, adored by her teachers and classmates alike, and showed such remarkable qualities that a stage career was soon accepted as a foregone conclusion.

A dancer's career in Italy in the mid-nineteenth century held the promise of exciting rewards, for there was a long and distinguished tradition of ballet which had taken root in the many cities that were or had at one time been capitals of small kingdoms, principalities and duchies. Opera and ballet constituted the normal fare of theatres throughout the peninsula, not as a rarified culture implanted for an intellectual or social elite, but accepted naturally by all the strata of the theatre-going public. The proportion of performances of opera and ballet was much greater in Italy than elsewhere in Europe. Opera was very much a native form, but ballet had also flourished naturally and with a markedly different aesthetic than applied in France.

The work of Salvatore Viganò and Gaetano Gioja in Milan and Salvatore Taglioni in Naples had established a tradition of Italian choreography that rested on strongly dramatic plots and powerfully rendered interpretations. Since gesture played a greater part in ordinary communication among Italians than with the more restrained peoples to the north, it is not surprising that mime should figure much more prominently in Italian ballet. There had been times when this was carried to the extreme where the roles in a ballet were played by mimes, leaving the principal dancers to appear only in incidental *pas*, but by Virginia's day Italian choreographers were devoting more attention to the dance, and the leading ballerina was invariably expected to play the heroine of the action.

At the outset of Virginia's career these traditions were being worthily followed by skilful and prolific choreographers such as Giuseppe Rota, Pasquale Borri and the Italianised Frenchman, Ippolito Monplaisir, in whose ballet *Brahma* she was to gain one of her greatest triumphs. These men led peripatetic existences, travelling among the many theatres in Italy that competed for their services. The Italian theatrical industry was organised on a seasonal basis. While a theatre would maintain a permanently employed administration and a basic company, productions were planned for the season and the star singers and dancers engaged on short-term contracts. The most important season was always that of Carnival and Lent, which opened traditionally on St. Stephen's Day, December 26th, and continued until shortly before Easter. Other seasons took place in the summer and the autumn, but less money was spent on these and lower standards were tolerated. With the proliferation of theatres offering opera and ballet Italian choreographers had a wide field of opportunity, and their most successful ballets were produced all over the peninsula, not only by their creators but also by lesser ballet-masters who specialised in reproductions.

Another source of strength in Italian ballet lay in the brilliant technique that was taught, particularly at the School of Ballet at La Scala. There had been a time when the best talent had to be imported and the leading dancers, whatever their nationality,

were generally referred to as the *coppia di rango francese*, but by
the 1860s the Italian school had become paramount throughout
Europe for its technical accomplishments. Carlo Blasis, who
directed the School of Ballet of La Scala from 1837 to 1850, had
introduced a method that produced an impressive succession of
virtuosos, including Sofia Fuoco, Amalia Ferraris, Caterina Beretta,
Carolina Pochini and many others who won international fame.
Virginia Zucchi, though not a product of the Scala School, was no
doubt trained according to the same method, for she, too,
developed into a technician of not inconsiderable prowess.

    According to Valerian Svetlov, who knew her well during
her visits to Russia, her parents placed her in a wandering troupe of
child performers, where she gained her first stage experience at the
same time that she was receiving her early lessons in dancing. If this
was true, no record has survived of it. It is more likely that she em-
barked on her career as a soloist in the minor theatres of northern
Italy. Her debut* took place in 1864 in the little theatre at Varese.
Watched from the wings by an anxious mother who still found it
difficult to reconcile herself to having a professional dancer as a
daughter, she appeared, in a purely dancing role, in a ballet by
Francesco Razzani called *Nisa, ossia Lo spirito danzante.* For some
years Signora Zucchi hardly ever let her child out of sight, protect-
ing her with possessive vigilance from the attentions of the young
bloods who flocked around her. Virginia, however, was a sensible
and well balanced girl, and her head was not to be turned by the
superficial glitter of the theatre nor by the flattery and adulation
that surrounded her as she began to build up a modest reputation.

*A Virginia Zucchi was listed among the sixteen *prime ballerine di mezzo
carattere* in the company of the Scala, Milan, during the Carnival season of
1863, but this was more likely a namesake, Virginia Amalia Zucchi—apparently unrelated—who danced in Bologna in the winter of 1865, in Nice early in
1867, and as *prima ballerina assoluta* in Trieste in the autumn season of 1869.

Her next reported engagement was at the Teatro Contavelli
in Bologna, where she appeared in a mediocre ballet by Francesco
Magri called *Gabriella di Nancy* in March 1865. From there, in the
early summer, she went to Reggio in Emilia as one of two *prime
ballerine assolute.* Being still a beginner, she willingly accepted the
seniority of her more experienced colleague, Marina Mori, but even
in the less prominent roles that were assigned to her she created a
strong impression that earned her an engagement, for the autumn
season, at the Teatro di Borgognissanti in Florence.

This time she was billed as the first of the two *prime ballerine assolute,* and in Ludovico Pedroni's ballet *Jankee*—a topical
work, no doubt, for the American Civil War had only recently
ended—her precocious talent was so skilfully contrasted with the
more mature style of Adele Paglieri that the public split into rival
camps and contested the superiority of their favourites with a
passion that Florence had not known for years. One critic found
the clamour quite disconcerting. "The spectator who goes to form
a true judgment on the merits of these dancers," he declared,
"will leave the theatre so stunned and bruised that instead of
awarding the apple to the more beautiful, or rather the more skilful, he will take it home and eat it with his family!"[3]

Another critic threw caution to the winds and boldly declared himself to be "a devoted Zucchino. What does it matter,"
he went on, "if that light little devil called Virginia Zucchi is not
irreproachable in everything? What enchants me about her is just
what charmed Pellico, *'il gato spirto de' suoi giovani anni,'* adolescence combined with the studies of the artist, a girl's gentle man-
ners made more delightful and attractive by the precocious
development of the forms of womanhood, an artistic instinct that
is neither instilled nor acquired, and the quality which makes a
woman, especially if she be an artist, an absolute sovereign, a fairy
queen whose kingdom has no bounds."[4]

In the following year, 1866, she accepted engagements at
Piacenza and Ferrara and in the autumn returned to Bologna to

take part in a production of Meyerbeer's opera *Roberto il Diavolo.*
Presumably she was cast as the Abbess in the Ballet of the Nuns, a
role created by Taglioni that would have enabled her to reveal her
natural gift for expression. The critic of *L'Arpa* mentioned her
as "the excellent dancer, Virginia Zucchi, for whom we predict
the most splendid career."[5]

The Teatro Comunale in Trieste, where she danced during
the Carnival and Lent season of 1866–67, marked a new stage in
her progress. It was her first foreign engagement, for Trieste, although possessing a predominantly Italian population, lay across
the frontier in the Austrian Empire. Nevertheless the Comunale
was to all intents and purposes an Italian theatre, presenting seasons of opera and ballet just as if it had been situated in the heart
of Italy. Virginia found herself billed second in order of importance,
preceded by Angelina Fioretti, an Italian ballerina of considerable
distinction who had danced at the Paris Opéra. The season opened
disastrously with a wretched reproduction of Paul Taglioni's
comedy ballet *Flik e Flok*, in which Virginia nervously but successfully appeased the audience's bad humour with a spirited polka.
When the ballet was dropped, the dancers restored their honour
with a brilliant *pas de trois* which Alessandro Rossi-Brighenti produced for himself, Fioretti and Virginia. Matters could only improve after such a bad start; the next production, Andrea
Palladino's *Benvenuto Cellini,* was better received, and the season
ended with an excellent reproduction of another ballet by Paul
Taglioni, *Leonilda.*

From Trieste Virginia sailed down the Adriatic coast to
Zara to appear in a ballet by Vianello called *Vasco di Gama.* It was
largely a personal triumph. Every evening she received a dozen curtain calls, the applause reaching heights of frenzy after a Scottish
dance which she performed, characteristically, "with great feeling
and a vivacious sensuality of movement."[6] Her next engagement,
in the autumn of 1867, was at the Teatro Nazionale in Florence,
where once again she came to the rescue by calming a restive audi-

ence. It was only her arch rendering of the she-devil heroine that redeemed the utter mediocrity of Giovacchino Coluzzi's ballet, *Bedra la Maliarda.*

Her reputation was now spreading throughout the north of Italy, and the Carnival and Lent season of 1867–68 found her in Turin, then the nation's capital, dancing at the Teatro Regio in a company headed by Emilia Laurati. Antonio Pallerini was the choreographer, and Virginia danced with success in his ballets, *La Grotta d'Adelberga, Zelia* and *Nyssa e Saib.* Her popularity in Turin assumed such proportions that, when the season at the Regio ended, she moved to the Teatro Balbo as the principal ballerina, delighting the Torinese public for several weeks longer in a series of ballets by Ferdinando Pratesi: *I Quattro Caratteri, Lionilla* and *Un Patto infernale. Lionilla* provided an impressive test of her stamina, for the leading part required her to be on stage almost throughout, and yet she seemed as fresh at the end as at the beginning. As a measure of her growing reputation, she was given a benefit performance—her first—at the Teatro Balbo, and from all reports it was highly successful. "The theatre was illuminated, the audience packed tight," described a journalist present; "there were flowers and colossal bouquets, very elegant and unusual ribbons, cheers, applause—it was something extraordinary!"[7]

A few minor engagements followed that summer: at Busseto, for the inauguration of the Teatro Verdi, where she danced in a modest ballet by Provinciali, *Un Casino all'incante,* and a few weeks later, at the Teatro Municipale in Casale, where she appeared in Pratesi's *Un Patto infernale.* The early months of 1869 found her at Brescia and Verona, receiving ovations in a ballet called *La Lorette,* not only for her dancing but also for her dramatic rendering of a mad scene that the ballet contained. From these triumphs she was to move to centres of greater importance and to pass two milestones that were to prove significant in her progress as a ballerina. In the summer of 1869 she accepted a short engagement at the Politeama Fiorentino in Florence, where she appeared in a dramatic ballet called *Rolla*, the work of a young and virtually unknown choreographer, Luigi Manzotti. She may have sensed his unusual promise, but she was not to know that in later years his ballets were to bring her triumphs in Paris and Milan. Nor was he, at this first crossing of their paths, to perceive her dramatic gifts, for she played no part in the action, appearing merely in a *pas de deux* with Arturo Viganò. The second symbolic milestone appeared very shortly afterwards, at the Teatro Vittorio Emanuele in Turin, where Giuseppe Bini reproduced several well-known ballets: *La Contessa d'Egmont* and *Lo Spirito maligno* by Giuseppe Rota, Saint-Léon's *Fiamma d'amore,* and −most significant of all−*Esmeralda.*

    Esmeralda was one of the most popular ballets that had come down from the Romantic period. Created a quarter of a century before by Jules Perrot, it was a powerful rendering in dance and mime of Victor Hugo's novel, *Notre Dame de Paris,* and the title role had given scope for two very different interpretations, the gentle rendering of Carlotta Grisi and, overshadowing it, the gripping dramatic characterisation that Fanny Elssler had made of it. In the few performances which Virginia gave in Turin she "shone with extraordinary brilliance": "as a ballerina she surpassed herself, while as a mime she was a revelation because nobody had expected such boldness and passion from her."[8] Her interpretation was of course still only a sketch of what it was to become later in her career, when her Esmeralda was to take its place, in the annals of ballet, alongside that of Elssler as a supreme example of the skill of a dancer-actress.

    Her lengthy stay in Turin won her many admirers, and not surprisingly the curiosity of King Victor Emmanuel was soon aroused. Examining the young dancer through his opera glasses one evening, the king, whose eye for the ladies was implicit in his nickname of *"il re galant'uomo"*, was so taken with her beauty and shapely form that a *régisseur* was commanded to go to her dressing room in the interval with a discreet invitation to supper after the performance. The innocent Virginia was thrown into a state of confusion, and her astute and watchful mother at once realised that some proposition had been received. When challenged, Virginia was too abashed to disclose the source of the invitation, and she allowed herself to be taken back to her lodgings like a wayward child. Next day all Milan seemed to know about the incident, but Signora Zucchi was unrepentant; she would sooner withdraw her daughter from the stage altogether, she declared, than allow her to have supper with an admirer, even if it were the King.

It was inevitable, of course, that sooner or later this maternal vigilance would relax, and that Virginia would break free from this tutelage. The story of her first love, when it came, had all the trappings of true romance. It began one evening when a jewel casket and bouquet were delivered to her dressing room with the card of Emmanuel Albert, Count of Mirafiori. This new admirer was the illegitimate son of the King by his mistress, Rosa Vercellana, and was some two years younger than Virginia. Brought up to be wary of valuable gifts, Virginia dutifully returned the casket. But Emmanuel Albert was not to be rebuffed so easily. The very next day he paid a call on the Zucchis, bearing the rejected casket. He turned out to be a young man of great charm—he was described by an Austrian diplomat as "one of the handsomest and most clean-limbed Italians" he had ever met[9] —and in a very short time he conquered Virginia's formidable mother and left the house that day with permission to call again. The assiduous court which he paid to Virginia soon became public knowledge and, as Signora Zucchi's strict vigilance was equally well-known, it was widely believed that the two young people were engaged. Virginia had indeed fallen deeply in love, and she went to sleep with the bouquet of violets he had placed in her hair resting on her pillow.

Then, on a summer's night, taking advantage of a few clear days between performances, the couple eloped. On her return from this idyll, Virginia had to face her father's anger and her mother's reproaches and was made to promise never to see the young man

again. Meanwhile Emmanuel Albert had received an urgent summons to Turin, where his father, the King, was seriously ill. From
there he wrote to Virginia every day, but in obedience to her parents' wishes she left his letters unanswered. When she discovered
she was pregnant, however, her parents relented and realistically
accepted Emmanuel Albert as their daughter's protector.

   Virginia was forced to abandon the stage for a while. She
was unable to fulfil an engagement at the Teatro Argentina in
Rome, and some time in 1870 she gave birth to a daughter, who
was named Rosina after Emmanuel Albert's mother. When she was
well enough, she began to take daily class again. Later she claimed
that she gave up her career for some years, but this was an exaggeration. Towards the end of 1870 she was dancing at the Teatro La
Pergola in Florence, where she gained an unexpected triumph in
Ondina, taking over the title role at short notice after Carolina
Pochini had mistimed a jump and fallen into the prompter's box.
Emmanuel Albert wanted her to renounce the theatre altogether
and, had their life together run smoothly, she might have done so.
But his unfaithfulness led her to leave him, and she accepted an
engagement in Messina for the Carnival and Lent season of
1871–72. There, in a ballet by Giovanni Pulini called *Kamil*, she
savoured again the exhilarating ovations of the public, while back
in Turin Emmanuel Albert was beginning to fret at her absence.
After a few weeks he could bear his solitude no longer and turned
up hopefully in Messina. His presence did not pass unnoticed and,
one evening when he was in the theatre, a section of the audience
hissed Virginia on her entrance. He felt this as a personal affront,
and turning to General della Rocca, who was with him, he heatedly
exclaimed: "The fools think they are hissing just a dancer. Tomor-
row she will be my wife."

   His mother, however, had more ambitious plans for him.
He was recalled to Turin, and shortly afterwards Virginia received
an offer of 50,000 francs for the return of his letters. She refused
and, when the price was raised, returned the same answer. "I will

return these souvenirs of our love," she wrote to him, "if you ask
for them yourself. Surely it is not you who have allowed me to be
insulted?" The Count assured her that he had had no part in this.
He left her with the letters, confessing that pressure to marry was
being brought on him that it was difficult in his situation to resist.
He begged Virginia in vain not to break their association. She even
refused an offer of an allowance and returned his letters, asking
only that he never visit the theatre when she was dancing, for she
could not answer for her reactions if she knew he was watching
her. This promise he faithfully kept. The King wished to make a
settlement on Rosina, but Emmanuel Albert would not hear of it
and instead sold his magnificent stable of horses and made Virginia
a gift of the proceeds. Their romance did not end in bitterness.
Virginia made the sword knot in blue and gold thread which he
wore at his wedding, and afterwards he always wrote to her when
he required a new one, refusing to wear any that had not been
made by her hands.[10]

Virginia was left with her little daughter to recall the bliss
of her first love—a precious gift that was to be snatched from her
all too soon, for the child was delicate and died at the age of eight.
In later years she often looked back wistfully on her happy days
with Emmanuel Albert and freely confessed that she would have
abandoned the stage to marry him. From her private loss the dance
was to reap an immeasurable gain.

Spreading Fame

Rosina was presumably entrusted to the care of her grandparents, for Virginia continued her career after returning to the stage at Messina. Remaining for a while in Sicily—at the request, it seems, of the King—she danced at the Teatro del Circo in Palermo for two seasons, autumn 1872 and Carnival and Lent 1872–73, before returning north to Padua. There she was engaged at the Teatro Nuovo for the Fiera del Santo, a season of special festivity honouring the town's patron saint, St. Anthony of Padua. The ballet was under the direction of Ippolito Monplaisir, one of the foremost choreographers in Italy, who was to revive his celebrated dramatic ballet, *Brahma*. This work had been created at the Scala, Milan, in 1868 with Amalia Ferraris as the slave-girl Padmana, and now, for the Padua production, another internationally renowned ballerina, Claudina Cucchi, was to play the part. To a dancer of Cucchi's eminence Virginia had no objection to taking second place.

    Brahma, which was to figure prominently in her career, was a ballet in seven acts and a prologue, with a score by a brilliant young composer, Constantino Dall'Argine. Its plot traces the quest of the god Brahma for a pure and disinterested love, through which he can gain readmittance to Paradise. He descends to earth to find himself first in Nankin during the Festival of the Sacred Dragon. He pays the taxes of a wretched old man who has a beautiful daughter, but realises that the love the girl might feel for him would be tainted by gratitude. His attention is then drawn to a mandarin's daughter, but he perceives that her seductive charms conceal an inconstant heart. His wanderings take him to India,

21

where he buys a Parsee slave girl, Padmana, from an inkeeper. Padmana accompanies Brahma to the Dutch Indies, where, at the Viceroy's ball, his advances are haughtily rejected by the Viceroy's daughter and Padmana arouses the desires of Heder-Ali, chief of the Thugs. Resuming their journey, Brahma and Padmana lie down to rest in a forest, unaware that they are in a holy place where a remnant of the persecuted Parsee sect has established a temple. They are discovered. The penalty for such sacrilege is death, but Padmana is recognised as a former priestess of Zoroaster. She saves her master by sending the Parsees to consult the auguries. They flee into the jungle, pursued by Heder-Ali. They believe they have eluded him by mingling with a passing caravan, but they are ambushed and taken captive. Heder-Ali gives Padmana to the governor Soubah, who tries in vain to make her submit to his desires. In a dramatic scene Soubah threatens Brahma with death if Padmana will not yield. With a superhuman effort Brahma breaks his chains and, snatching a dagger from a guard, throws himself at Soubah. Brahma is disarmed and led away to be tortured, while Padmana stretches out her arms to him. In the last act a funeral pyre has been prepared. Overwhelmed with despair, Padmana is forced to take part in the funeral rites. Brahma mounts the pyre and, seeking Padmana in the crowd, gives her a sign of farewell. As the flames rise up, Padmana struggles free and, climbing the pyre, clasps Brahma in her arms to share his fate. The onlookers are awed by such a sacrifice. In the final apotheosis Brahma is seen ascending to Paradise with the girl who has given him the true love that is worthy of his immortality.

The role of Padmana was central to the action, but Ferraris had not brought out its dramatic possibilities at the Scala, nor did Cucchi measure up to it in Padua. Then, as if by a stroke of fate, Cucchi fell ill after a few performances and Virginia was given her chance. It was a daunting task to assume such a demanding role at short notice, and her performance could have been no more than a sketch of the interpretation that she was later to develop. But there

was enough in it to rouse the public to a high pitch of enthusiasm.
"What an evening!" exclaimed a French critic who was present.
"Never in my life have I been present on such a festive occasion,
even in Italy, which seems to have preserved the cult of its former
Gods for the goddesses of the stage and now sacrifices flowers as it
used to sacrifice victims. La Zucchi received all these tributes with
such exquisite grace and such a sweet smile that we were desperate
that we had not done more."[1]

In the course of time Virginia's interpretation of Padmana
was to become much richer and deeper. To a ballet that was otherwise not specially remarkable she was to add a new dimension of
dramatic expression by developing this role to a degree that made it,
in the true sense of the term, a work of her own creation. Much was
to be added later—notably, the famous scene when Padmana holds
the priests at bay by the fury of her look—but the seeds were sown
in Padua in the summer of 1873.

Engagements now followed rapidly. In August 1873, on
Monplaisir's recommendation, she was in Spoleto, dancing in his *La
Semiramide del Nord*. From there she went to the Teatro Apollo,
Rome, for the autumn season, to appear in *Idea*, a ballet by
Pasquale Borri. For the Carnival and Lent season of 1873–74 she ac-
companied Borri to the Teatro Carlo Felice in Genoa, where she
danced in two more of his ballets, *La Dea del Valhalla* and *Lionna*.

Virginia was now twenty-five and had been dancing as a
prima ballerina for nine years. As her reputation had grown, so had
the importance of her engagements and the geographical area of her
activities. Now, in the autumn of 1874, she achieved her ambition
to appear on the most celebrated stage in all Italy, that of the Scala,
Milan. Monplaisir was that season's choreographer, and it was in his
ballet *Estella*, with music by Paolo Giorza, that she made her
Milanese debut on September 13th, 1874. *Estella* was a light work
that had originally been produced eight years before for the more
popular stage of the Canobbiana, and was hardly appropriate for
the Scala. Set in the outskirts of Paris in the late eighteenth century,

it told the story of a young girl who is abducted by a cynical roué
and a courtesan for the pleasure of the young Count Enrico. The
Count has better feelings, however, and is so moved by the girl's
purity that he asks her to marry him, and the ballet ends with a
Festival of Roses.

This slight piece received harsh treatment from the critics,
even by the lower standards which they applied during the autumn
season, and Virginia's reception suffered in consequence. "La
Zucchi," reported *La Fama* condescendingly, "is a pleasant dancer
who does not yet aspire to the laurels of the famous, but can earn
applause in a season when the audience does not have the right to
demand Carnival performances."[2] She did, however, lift the ballet
above the level of mediocrity, particularly in a spectacular *pas de
deux* in which she was to be remembered most vividly by a dancer
who knew her at the time. "She was not only a ballerina with
pointes of steel," this dancer recalled. "She was an artist whose
resources had no limits. It is quite impossible to convey in words
her *pas de deux* in Monplaisir's *Estella*. You must have seen it for
yourself and thrown your whole heart behind that irresistible figure.
And remember that there had been a whole series of fiascos at the
Scala and there would have been a great outcry if she had not been
there."[3]

If the ballet had been disappointing, her personal success
was such that she was honoured with an invitation to return to the
Scala for the Carnival and Lent season of 1875–76. This time she
found herself working under Luigi Manzotti, who, like her, had
made significant progress since their paths had first crossed in
Rome six years before. Manzotti was a natural genius. The son of a
Milanese fruit-seller, he used to slip away from his father's stall to
visit the theatre. He was fascinated by the art of gesture and its ap-
plication to the stage, and he had eventually managed to enter
Giuseppe Bocci's mime class at the Scala. Then, having learnt as
much as he could there, he had gained experience as a mime in
Florence and Rome. During the fourteen years he had spent in

Rome he had read widely and produced his early ballets, including *Rolla* and *Pietro Micca.*

Recognition had now come to him, as it also had to Virginia, in the form of an engagement at the Scala for the important season of Carnival and Lent; and his ballet *Rolla* was presented, in a spectacular new production, on the opening night, December 26th, 1875. Its setting was Florence in the sixteenth century. Rolla, a young sculptor, is in love with Eleanora, but her father, an exiled politician, wishes to marry her to the influential Marchese Appiani in the hope of thereby regaining his lost fortune. Rolla wins the admiration of Michelangelo, who has come to judge a sculpture competition. Eleanora's father persuades the young artist to renounce his love and withdraw from the competition. In a fit of mad despair Rolla smashes his statue, but he is nonetheless awarded the prize on condition that he remake the statue. But it is too late: his mind has given way, and he dies in the arms of Michelangelo and Eleanora. In this ballet Virginia was cast not as Eleanora but as Elvira, who hoped to marry Appiani but generously restrains her jealousy when Eleanora appears as her rival, and in the end intercedes on Eleanora's behalf. Dramatically it was a part of secondary importance, and it was for her dancing that Virginia was to be remembered in this ballet—appearing, "agile, assured, and as precise as a chronometer"[4] in a brilliant *pas de deux* with Achille Coppini.

Her next role that season was in *La Sorgente*, a shortened version of the French ballet *La Source,* whose unpretentiousness was received as a welcome relief from the heavy choreographic dramas which were the usual fare at the Scala. The Milanese critics were beginning to warm to her, although so far they could only judge one side of her talent, for she had not yet been able to develop her dramatic flair. An appreciation which P. Cominazzi wrote in *La Fama* gave a revealing glimpse of her style. "The *pas* of Virginia Zucchi," he noted, "are astonishing for their vivacity and variety. Agility, flexibility, lightness, attack, strong *pointes*, sureness in *petite batterie* and turning are the gifts that dominate the style of

the charming ballerina who, in her difficult vocation, showed herself indefatigable and the possessor of marvellous strength in her
charming little body. A little more grace and a little more elegance. . .would not come amiss, but these are blemishes that
experience will smoothe away. The audience was fascinated by the
brio of her dancing and lost no opportunity to acclaim her."[5]

    She next appeared in a highly successful revival of Borri's
Il Figluol prodigo on March 26th and shortly afterwards, on April
8th, took the leading part in the *Dance of the Hours* divertissement
in Ponchielli's new opera, *La Gioconda.*

    It was a season of unusual brilliance. All the ballets were suc-
cessful, and in Manzotti the Scala had found a choreographer with
"fantasy, taste, true intelligence and an original touch."[6] The operatic offerings were no less impressive, the highlight being the Scala
debut in January of the Spanish tenor, Julián Gayarre, who later
created the role of Enzo in *La Gioconda.* With this "genius of song"
Virginia shared the laurels of the season. Their paths were to cross
again, with significant results, in years to come.

    With a Carnival triumph at the Scala behind her Virginia
found her status as a ballerina substantially enhanced. Her services
were more in demand than ever and not only by impresarios in Italy.
That summer her agent, Giuseppe Lamperti, negotiated an engagement at the Royal Opera in Berlin. For her this was a daunting
undertaking, for not only was it her first major foreign engagement,
but she had to learn no less than four new roles for the seven performances stipulated in the contract. Adding to the great consequence of this engagement was the renown of the venerable choreographer who was waiting for her in the German capital: Paul
Taglioni, son of the choreographer of *La Sylphide,* brother of the
greatest ballerina within living memory, and himself the creator of
a long series of successful ballets.

    For her first appearance he had chosen a role which she was
to play with conspicuous success throughout the remainder of her
career, Lise in *La Fille mal gardée.* This ballet was a survival from

the late eighteenth century, but Paul Taglioni had completely refurbished it in 1864, giving it new choreography of his own and a new score by Peter Ludwig Hertel, while retaining Dauberval's original scenario. During the rehearsal period Virginia found Taglioni a most exacting task-master. He was determined that her first entrance should be exactly as he wanted it and made her repeat it over and over again until she was reduced to despair.

"If I do not do it right this time," she vowed at last, "I will go away and never return."

Perhaps Taglioni heard her. At all events he declared himself satisfied by her next effort, and all was well.[7]

When she made her Berlin debut on May 13th, 1876, the critics regarded her with special interest, as a contender for the vacant post of prima ballerina. In the light of her reputation as a mime they were a little disappointed that a light, comic ballet such as *La Fille mal gardée* should have been chosen for her first appearance, and they judged her more for her qualities as a dancer. A passage of *pointe* work that she performed "as though walking on a telegraph wire" created a considerable sensation, but one critic "missed that graceful swing of the upper body."[8] In *Sardanapal,* which followed on the 18th, the emphasis in the reviews was again on the strength and stamina of her dancing. Her third ballet was *Madeleine,* Paul Taglioni's most recent work, a disguised and bowdlerised version of *Manon Lescaut,* and on June 6th she played the part of Topaze in *Flick und Flock.*

To appear in four new roles of contrasting character in a period of little more than three weeks would have been a formidable task under any circumstances. She could hardly have expected to develop these characterisations in any real depth, but the strain and the effort was too much even for her normally robust health. Her last performance before the season closed in June had to be cancelled, and it was not until the next season was some four weeks under way that she made her reappearance. For the next two years, until October 1878, Berlin was to be the main scene of her activity.

She appeared in several more ballets by Paul Taglioni, playing the title role in *Satanella*, and on November 12th, 1877, creating the part of the bayadère Zobeida in *Lamea,* a minor work to music selected from the scores of Delibes.

Unless the story she later told a French journalist was mere romancing for publicity's sake, she formed a strange relationship while she was in Berlin. A man of some eminence offered her his immense fortune if she would allow him to become her protector. For some months, while she held him at a distance, he showered her with gifts, demanding nothing in return, not even a kiss. She found this restraint most perplexing and, when she finally expressed her surprise with the intention of giving him some encouragement, "he paled, then blushed and finally fell ill." She lived with him for some months, during which he hardly ever left her and sighed many a deep sigh, but in the end she could stand this platonic union no longer and fled to Italy where, as she explained, "that type of man is not to be found." But after a few weeks a telegram reached her from her erstwhile friend's family, telling her that he was on the point of death and wished to see her once more before he died. She felt in duty bound to return to him, and two days after her arrival he died in her arms.[9]

This private drama did not interfere with her plans to visit Italy in the summer of 1877. News of her triumph in *La Fille mal gardée* had crossed the Alps before her, and the Teatro Dal Verme had invited her to give a short season in August. The ballet was staged for her by José Mendez, who specialised in reproducing the ballets of Paul Taglioni, and followed Verdi's *Macbeth* on the bill. The opera had only a modest success, but the ballet was a triumph for all concerned. The critics were unanimous in their praise for Virginia, who roused the audience to great enthusiasm, particularly in the *pas de ruban*, which she invariably had to repeat at later performances. Caterina Beretta, a retired ballerina who had become one of the most distinguished ballet teachers in Italy, went backstage to congratulate her and called her *"une fille bien réussie."*

Virginia had now had time to think out the character of
Lise, and her interpretation had gained such depth that it might have
been created specially for her. "She possesses to a high degree,"
wrote one critic, "the two qualities that are all-important in ballet—
elegance of person and movement, and good taste. Not one of her
variations is ever marred by anything acrobatic or grotesque, but
they all bring out the harmonious and charming lines of her graceful,
slender, well built and always elegant figure. Her gracefulness never
becomes affected or mawkish; her smile is a real smile and never the
stereotyped grimace learnt in class. She was truly admirable in all the
little caprices, fits of temper and pranks of the vivacious heroine, and
in the love scene her face expressed all those unconscious bewilder-
ments, those instinctive apprehensions, those sudden abandons that
the first thrill of sensual pleasure awakens in the inexperienced heart
and untouched limbs of a girl in the throes of her first love."[10]

In the state of mind that the strange platonic affair with the
Berlin admirer had left her, it is not surprising—again, if we are to
believe her own confession—that she succumbed willingly to a more
ardent lover. He was an Italian architect, who, as she put it herself,
regarded the word "love" as an active verb. He was also something
of a poet, and after each performance he sent her a mass of flowers
with a card bearing some gallant message. With the typical hyperbole
of a Latin lover, he claimed that Virginia possessed the soul of
Dante in the body of a Titian and that the Mussulmans would abandon the houris of their Paradise if she were to dance in the temple of
Mecca on a feast day. But there was one obstacle to their bliss—the
architect's wife, who one day most disagreeably invaded their little
nest in the country. Virginia fled, and next day all Milan seemed to
know of her confrontation with the outraged wife. She denied the
story and tried to brave it out by appearing in a box at the theatre.
But she had not counted on the architect and his wife, now apparently reconciled, occupying the box immediately opposite. Her
embarrassment can be imagined, and she was glad of an excuse to
escape from Milan.

After two seasons in Berlin she felt in need of a change, and
an offer to dance at the Royal Italian Opera, Covent Garden, came
at a most opportune moment. There was, however, one difficulty
which cost her a tremendous effort of will to overcome. She had a
morbid terror of the sea, and she insisted on a condition permitting
her to remain at Calais for as long as the Channel was rough. But a
change of scene was imperative, for reasons that were more weighty
than the annoying tittle-tattle of Milan. In the space of a few months
she had suffered two bereavements—the deaths of her mother and
her daughter Rosina—and now, seeking consolation in her art, she
summoned up the courage to carry her across the English Channel.
    An added attraction perhaps of this London engagement
was that Julián Gayarre, the handsome Spanish tenor, would be
singing at Covent Garden while she was there. Her Italian *inamorato*
receded a little into the background, but only a few days after her
arrival she learnt of his death. According to her own story, he had
committed suicide by wrenching out, with his own hands, the key-
stone of a bridge he had designed and falling to his end amid the
rubble.
    At Covent Garden the dance occupied a very minor place in
the programmes, and Virginia, who had arrived towards the end of
the 1878 season, created little stir. Her first appearance was on June
10th in a short ballet divertissement by Joseph Hansen. The few
critics who troubled to write about her London debut noted not
only her physical attraction and her technical accomplishments but
also her "piquant and expressive" miming. Later she was seen in
the skating ballet in Meyerbeer's *Le Prophète* and a carnival ballet
interpolated in Flotow's opera *Alma l'Incantatrice.* A report of her
success in London, published in the *Gazzetta Musicale di Milano,*
that compared it with the triumphs of Cerrito, Taglioni and Elssler,
was certainly exaggerated, but she was welcomed back to Covent
Garden for the last few weeks of the 1879 season when, as well as
Le Prophète, she danced in incidental divertissements in Ambroise
Thomas' *Hamlet* and Massenet's *Le Roi de Lahore.*

A full year was to pass before her next engagement. Returning to Paris, she interrupted her career to give birth to her second child. In the early hours of December 10th, 1879, she was delivered of a baby girl who was baptised with the name of Marie. The father of the child was Adolphe Henri David Jourdan, an importer for French companies in Italy and also a painter of some repute. He was twenty-four years older than Virginia, and at the time of his death, in 1889, he held the post of Director of the School of Drawing at Nîmes.

Virginia had no intention of abandoning her career, and the autumn of 1880 found her on the boards again, at the Politeama in Rome. She was now thirty-one, and her dramatic genius was coming into full flower. This was evident in the rather insipid part she played in *La Semiramide del Nord*, but its extraordinary range was revealed most tellingly in the contrast between *La Fille mal gardée* and *Brahma*. In this latter ballet she had developed the role of Padmana into a powerful characterisation that reached a climax of breath-taking tension in the daggers scene. At her benefit performance she had to repeat both this scene and that of Padmana's death, and the audience's enthusiasm reached such proportions that there was a time when the whole stage seemed to be covered with flowers thrown from the auditorium.

For the opening of the Carnival season of 1880–81 at the Teatro San Carlo in Naples Cesare Marzagora staged a brilliant production of *La Sorgente*, in which she made a stunning first impression. The critic of *Pungolo* extolled her "beauty, grace, strength and bravura, added to very mobile features that many an actress would envy," and called her "the dancer's ideal."[12] It was a splendid beginning. A few days afterwards Amina Boschetti, a celebrated ballerina of an earlier generation who was to produce one of the season's ballets, died unexpectedly of a heart attack. Her funeral was attended by almost the entire ballet company of the San Carlo, and Virginia's presence in one of the carriages did not pass unnoticed. This mark of respect stood her in good stead, and she re-

ceived a vociferous ovation when she appeared in her next role, in
La Fille mal gardée.

But all this good work was soon to be undone. To replace
Boschetti's ballet the management called upon Caterina Beretta to
stage a revival of *Brahma.* Virginia, whose contract was for Carnival
only, assumed that her engagement would be extended through
Lent to enable her to dance in the ballet which she had elsewhere
almost made her own, but to her consternation she was passed over
in favour of the virtually unknown Giovannina Limido, Beretta's
favourite pupil. Nor was this all. The young dancer gained a great
personal triumph, in spite of the shortcomings of the hastily substi-
tuded production.

Most injudiciously Virginia tried to vent her displeasure by
encouraging, or at least condoning, a demonstration at the second
performance. Commenting on the disturbance, a critic wrote:
"There can be no doubt that this most disgraceful uproar. . . was
entirely the work of Signora Zucchi, who was exceedingly jealous
of the tumultuous success obtained by her colleague, Signora
Limido. In fact only a handful of idle subscribers took part in that
evening's incident. They achieved nothing beyond frightening away
a few ladies. . . and afterwards receiving an unwelcome visit from
the police, and their main purpose—to bring down the curtain and
thus make *Brahma* a failure and force the management either to
close the theatre or re-engage the fascinating *'fille BIEN gardée'* —
was thwarted. . . . Seeing the humiliating reverse suffered by her le-
gion, Signora Zucchi thought it wise to beat a prudent retreat and,
although she yearned to make her final appearance in *Brahma,* she
left a day or two later without a word of farewell."[13]

In this unfortunate affair Virginia, it seems, was led astray
by her young brother Vittorio, who instigated the disturbance. It
was perhaps not the first time he had done her a disservice by his
headstrong championing of her interests, for a report of this incident
in Naples pointedly referred to him as "her notorious brother."[14]

Her reputation suffered considerably, and a sour note was
detectable in the reports of her engagements over the next twelve

months. At the Teatro Constanzi, Rome, she had a somewhat reserved reception in *La Fille mal gardée* during the summer of 1881. From there she returned to Milan, where she was engaged at the Dal Verme for the Carnival season of 1881–82. Once again she found herself in direct competition with Giovannina Limido, who was making her debut at the Scala in Marzagora's new ballet *Daï-Natha.* Virginia was at a decided disadvantage, for the Dal Verme lacked the resources, both in money and in personnel, that were at the disposal of the Scala. In consequence *Brahma,* in which she made her first appearance, was meagrely produced in comparison to the lavish staging of Daï-Natha, which also had an Indian setting; but in spite of all this the public flocked to see her, drawn by reports of her astonishing daggers scene.

A critic, who signed himself "Lo Sbarazzino" (the urchin), wrote a vivid description of Virginia Zucchi as he saw her for the first time on that opening night at the Dal Verme. He was bewitched from the very moment of her first entrance, when she advanced to the front of the stage to acknowledge the audience's ovation with a dignified smile.

This was how she appeared to him: "Of medium height, black hair lightly curled and falling on to the shoulders, a broad forehead that bespeaks a 'superior intellect', eyes that are very black and Jewish, shaded by thick eyebrows, and flashing with strange gleams, round cheeks, a mouth that is most graceful, a short chin, Junoesque shoulders, a full bust, well shaped arms, broad hips, legs that are tense and very strong, small feet.

"Her dancing is like embroidery, a mixture of difficulties effortlessly overcome and the greatest fluidity; in short a combination of agility, originality and lightness that leaves the spectator astonished.

"The now famous scene of the daggers in *Brahma* is a creation of the eminent artist. . . . You see her playing ingenuously with her shadow while Brahma, exhausted by his journey, takes a little repose. She looks around with anxious apprehension, fearing that some danger is in store for her divine lover. She listens intently, looks about her, and finally sits down at the feet of her beloved.

"Meanwhile in the jungle the priests are already stirring, their daggers raised to strike down the outcast from Paradise. Zucchi, we have no hesitation in saying, is a great artist in this dramatic episode. . . .

"Like a wild lioness she leaps to her feet, terrible and fascinating. She raises aloft her beautiful arms that, to quote Petrarch, are whiter than the snow that falls silently on the hillside and, pointing her finger at the sacrilegious priests, she commands them to begone, at the same time letting fall the cloak that covers her and revealing herself in all the beauty of a woman and a goddess.

"But the priests, hungry for blood, and bent on punishing him who has dared to profane the sacred mysteries of the jungle by his presence, return to the attack. In this scene, in which she again repels Brahma's enemies, Zucchi attains the very peak of the arts of mime and plastique.

"The fierce expressive eyes that shine like rubies in the dark, the sculptured pose of the body, the sublime rise and fall of her bosom, the imperious, regal gesture transport the spectator into the azure regions of the ideal, into a fairyland among the passionate sultanas of the *Thousand and One Nights*. . . ."[15]

The other ballet which she presented at the Dal Verme that season was not so successful. This was *La Giocoliera*, an old ballet of Pasquale Borri's which, in Zucchi's own reproduction, was now showing its age. The first scene, with its spirited tarantella, was pleasing enough, but after that the ballet languished and its fate was variously described as a semi-fiasco and a half-boiled success. Virginia performed her mime scenes, especially those that demanded passion, with great feeling and realism, but was criticised as a dancer for "resorting all too often to acrobatics that are ill suited to a 'dance celebrity' unless that title is downgraded to the level of the Dal Verme."[16] Be that as it may, the admiration of the Dal Verme

public almost amounted to idolatry, and one theatrical paper reported a new epidemic—acute Zucchitis!

When she danced in *La Fille mal gardée* at the Teatro
Grande, Brescia, in August 1882, it was clear that this epidemic was
spreading, and the Scala, Milan, decided that she could be ignored
no longer. She was engaged as *prima ballerina assoluta* for the
Carnival and Lent season of 1882–83, and two revivals went into
preparation: Ferdinando Pratesi's *L'Astro degli Afghan*, reproduced
by Cesare Smeraldi, and Luigi Manzotti's *Excelsior*. Both ballets
had music by Romualdo Marenco, but there the similarity ended.

L'Astro degli Afghan, in which Virginia made her first appearance of the season on January 3rd, 1883, was a ballet in the
conventional mould. The plot recounts the consequences of an
Afghan king's untimely death while his son is absent from the kingdom. On his return the young prince is in despair because he has
not heard his father's last wish, a matter that superstition holds to
be so grave that he is unwilling to ascend the throne. This wish is,
however, revealed to him by the intervention of Astreria, the guard-
ian spirit of the family. He then has to undergo a series of trials
and vicissitudes before he can become king. The prize is a beautiful
virgin, Even, daughter of a mountain chief. It is her appointed fate
to be sacrificed to the God of Fire, but the prince finally saves her
by making her his bride. The role of Even gave Virginia little opportunity for dramatic expression, but the production was impressive
and some of the scenes choreographically very effective, and the
ballet held its own until *Excelsior* was produced on February 19th.

Manzotti's *Excelsior* was the most astonishing and by far
the most successful spectacle that Italian ballet had ever produced.
Created at the Scala in January 1881, it had been performed there
more than one hundred times before the end of that year. Since
then it had been staged in Naples, Turin, Florence and Trieste, and
most recently Manzotti had gone to Paris to produce it for the
opening of the new Eden-Théâtre. It was quite unlike any other

ballet that had been produced. Instead of being based on one of
the typical themes of fantasy, historical drama or light comedy, it
was a colossal survey of the struggle between the forces of progress
and obscurantism, presenting the achievements of science, engineer-
ing and industry, and concluding with an apotheosis of Light and
Universal Peace. Nowadays it might appear naive and socially superficial, but in its day it was a serious attempt to break with escapist
themes and relate the art of ballet to the modern world. At the
same time it reflected society's comfortable, even complacent, assurance that the capitalist civilisation of Europe was progressing
inexorably towards better things and the hope that the nations
might at last settle down in a spirit of brotherhood. More than five
hundred dancers were utilised in the twelve scenes, which included
Volta's laboratory, the Central Telegraph Office in Washington, the
Suez Canal and the Mont Cenis tunnel. Virginia played the central
role of Civilisation.

       With its emphasis on spectacle and its lack of dramatic con-
tent, it was not a very suitable vehicle for her. Nor was it surprising
that certain critics preferred her predecessors in the role—Rosina
Viale, Adele Besesti, Albertina Flindt—even though Manzotti himself was satisfied enough to present her with a valuable crown as a
token of his regard. But there were other grounds for criticism. "I
do not approve of the new *pas* in the Suez scene," wrote the
Gazzetta dei Teatri, "and even less the performance of her part.
What seemed wholly unworthy of an artist of Zucchi's standing
were her costumes, which might have won a prize at a masked ball
at the Dal Verme but were horribly unbecoming in the strict and
decorous confines of art. I believe that even a second ballerina
would have disdained to bedeck herself in such a fashion and am
highly astonished that Manzotti and the management permitted for
her what for anyone else, and rightly so, they would certainly have
been quick to forbid."[17] The costumes were excessively extravagant. The critic of *Il Caricaturista* criticised them for being too re-

vealing and close-fitting, [18] and photographs show a staggering profusion of accessories that would have been more appropriate to a
variety theatre than to an opera house.

Virginia Zucchi was now a star of international magnitude.
Impresarios from far and wide clamoured for her services. Russia
was interested, and from Egypt came an offer of 60,000 francs a
year. But she refused them both, St. Petersburg for fear of the
cold, and Cairo for fear of the sea.

"I do not want a bridge of gold to cross the Mediterranean," she said. "A bridge of iron would suffice." [19]

So it was that an offer from closer at hand was accepted,
and in the summer of 1883 she set out to conquer Paris.

The Paris Eden

Virginia Zucchi's conquest of Paris has been immortalised in the large, full-length portrait by Georges Clairin which today looks down on the scholars and students working in the Bibliothèque de l'Opéra. There she stands, in the flush of triumph, posing proudly against a scenery flat on the stage of the Eden-Théâtre. The allure of her physical presence emanates strongly from the canvas. Her well-formed bust and her slim waist, so much admired in her day, her slim ankles and beautifully arched insteps are by any standards ravishing. Set in a strikingly light complexion, the green-hazel eyes that stirred her contemporaries look out with that compelling magnetism that once flashed across the great expanse of an auditorium, and her mouth, with its tendency to turn up at the corners, gives a challenging, quizzical expression to her features. Only in one respect has the painter toned down the individuality of his subject: he has, as it were, passed a comb through her unruly mane of hair that grew, thick, black and curly, to not much more than shoulder length. This was the ballerina that fascinated Paris in the winter of 1883–84.

Today the Eden-Théâtre has virtually passed from human memory, and few books on the history of ballet give it a mention. But at the outset of its brief existence, through its policy of presenting Italian ballet, it administered a shock to the French dance world that was little short of sensational. Constructed on the site of a large private mansion and its grounds in the Rue Boudreau, only a stone's throw from the Opéra, it was truly a monster of a theatre. To complete it the builders had made history by working

38

through the winter nights by electric light and, when the opening
was announced in January 1883, all Paris clamoured to see the
marvels that had been prepared behind the ornate exterior that
had risen up to fill the sixty-metre frontage. The Eden-Théâtre was
an amusement house rather than a theatre, for while the stage was
larger than that of the Opéra, the bizarrely decorated auditorium
(described by a journalist as "in the Egypto-Assyrio-Indian style")
occupied only part of the building. In addition to the immense
foyer that stretched the full width of the façade, there was a vast
Indian Court on one side and, on the other, a Winter Garden with
a grotto. Scattered through these halls were numerous bars—English, Dutch, American, Parisian, Spanish, Italian, Russian, Swiss—
each served by barmaids in appropriate national costume, and to
add atmosphere there was a Spanish guitarist and a quartet of
Tzigane musicians trying to make themselves heard.

Paris was accustomed to enjoying its ballet in association
with opera, while in London ballet had taken root in the music hall.
The management of the Eden offered a new permutation—Italian
ballet and the circus. For the circus acts, which opened the programme, a specially designed ring was lowered on to the stage from
the flies. The sensation of the opening night, however, was the
ballet that followed—Luigi Manzotti's *Excelsior*, which, by the
sheer scale of its production, dwarfed the ballets that were presented by the Opéra. Several hundred Italian dancers had been
gathered from all over Italy—the district surrounding the Eden had
become a veritable Italian colony—and in the ensemble scenes the
stage was filled with a seemingly incredible number of performers
who danced with a precision that was equally astonishing to Parisian eyes.

It was, above all, this discipline that created the sensational
impact. One critic commented that the ballet might have been
staged by the German General Staff and that he expected Field-
Marshal von Moltke to enter any moment on horseback. Others,
however, were so bedazzled by the spectacle and precision that,

in their effort to praise this new type of ballet, they denigrated the offerings of the Opéra—"those absurb scenarios," said one, "which show us the eternal Mérante, with his smile à la crême, trying to snatch a rose which Mlle. Sangalli or Mlle. Mauri obstinately hides from him."[1] It was to take a little time for the Parisians to recover a balanced view and to see that there was a world of difference between the two types of ballet and that no less admirable qualities were to be found in French ballet.

This was the background to Rita Sangalli's plaintive remark about the praise that was being lavished on Elena Cornalba, the Italian ballerina of the Eden: "But I do the same thing!"

So great was the success of *Excelsior* in Paris that it was performed at the Eden nightly to full houses during a run of over nine months. For the leading roles there were three separate casts, Cornalba sharing her burden with the Neapolitan Emma Palladino and Albertina Flindt, an American dancer from New Orleans. Cornalba, whom Virginia was to find as the ballerina in possession, was Milanese by birth and training, and the wife of the mime Egidio Rossi. In Paris she became a star overnight, with her extraordinary agility and suppleness, her dazzling turns, and, above all, her unprecedented *pointe* work. Some connoisseurs detected a lack of harmony between her tireless legs and the upper part of her body and criticised her for certain effects of doubtful taste. To believe one commentator, her appeal was almost that of an athlete rather than a dancer. "Never before," he wrote, "have I seen an automaton perform with such mathematical precision the steps which make up the restricted repertory of modern choreography— *battements, coupés, jetés, tours sur la pointe* without lowering the heel, *pointes en arrière, adages, sauts* and *pirouettes.* Cornalba performs these steps with the precision of a chronometer. America has given us the typewriter; exhibitions have accustomed us to mobile stoves, sewing machines and threshing machines. The Eden-Théâtre has now revealed the multi-point *entrechat* cutter, for this

amazing product that is going to revolutionise the French art of
the dance is none other than Cornalba, the patent dancer. But alas,
even the finest medal has its reverse side and, in spite of her immense talent, Cornalba lacks feminine charm—the smile, the love-
able gesture, a voluptuous flow in her movement—for cruel Nature
has endowed this dancer with legs of iron, *pointes* of steel, arms
of wood and the head of an English terrier."[2]

Some time during the summer of 1883 Virginia Zucchi arrived in Paris and began studying the title role of Manzotti's ballet
Sieba, which the choreographer was restaging, in an expanded
version, for her Paris debut.* *Sieba* had been first produced in
Turin five years before, in 1878, with Angelina Fioretti, and since
then had been successfully revived at the Scala, Milan, and elsewhere in Italy. The Eden production was planned on a gigantic
scale. The original work was expanded by several new numbers,
for which a composer called Venanzi was commissioned to write
the music to rhythms dictated by the choreographer, and advance
publicity whetted the appetite of the Paris public by hinting at
unprecedented scenic marvels, including a devil's sabbath scene, in
which three hundred persons were to take part, and a shipwreck.

Sieba was not only a more conventional type of ballet, to
French eyes, than *Excelsior*, but also much more of a ballerina's
ballet. In the episodic *Excelsior* the ballerina merely appeared in a
few highlighted numbers, but *Sieba* was constructed on a dramatic
narrative in which the ballerina developed the role of the heroine.
Although it opened with a scene set in Valhalla, in which the
valkyries, of whom Sieba is one, make their first entrance, it was
far removed from Wagner's opera. The plot hinged on the treacher-
ous attempt of Kafur, the prime minister of Thule, to seize the

*The Mlle. Zucchi who had appeared at the Skating-Rink in the Rue Blanche
in 1879–80, dancing in a series of ballets by Mariquita, was not Virginia but
her sister Costantina.

crown from the rightful king, Harold. The king invokes the aid of
the god Wodan in his struggle against the Gantars, and Sieba offers
to descend to earth to deliver the divine sword that will bring victory. She is warned that, if she should love a mortal, she will lose
her divinity and can never hope to enter Valhalla again. Kafur
manages to steal the sword, and the king is taken prisoner by
Danish pirates. Despite the warning, Sieba falls in love with Harold,
and on her return to Valhalla she is rejected and cast into the
Underworld. Wodan allows her to escape, for it is her fate now to
live among mortals. She is taken to the pirate ship, and there,
when Kafur treacherously gives the order for the king to be
killed, she throws herself into Harold's arms and, exposing Kafur
as a traitor, snatches the sword. The ship strikes a rock in a storm
and sinks; and the ballet ends with Harold presenting Sieba to his
people as his queen.

   Sieba replaced *Excelsior* on the stage of the Eden on
November 23rd, 1883, with Virginia Zucchi as the valkyrie.
Everyone was curious to see whether Manzotti would repeat his
earlier triumph. Inevitably the initial impression was not so great,
for the element of novelty was now lacking in the astonishing
precision of the large ensembles, but the critics bestowed great
praise on the lavish production. If there was a certain coldness
to be detected in the audience, that was attributed to a delay in
starting, the noisy score and the high price of seats.

   The novelty of Italian ballet still had the power to shock,
and reports of the new production were published in faraway
places where readers could not hope to see it for themselves.
Three thousand miles away, in New York, the *Spirit of the Times*
carried an informative paragraph. "It is not a style of dancing," it
explained, "that can for a moment be compared to the French
school—the sculptural musical dance that has its languor and
logical rhythms, the dance that softens and multiplies beauty,
the peculiarity of which is, as Jouffroy said, 'to make us imagine

souls by means of bodies.' The French dance is a plastic art, inas-
much as it unites within itself majesty of lines and variety of movement. The dancing at the Eden is to the dancing at the Opéra what
Grévin's impertinent silhouettes are to Baudry's decorative panels;
it is crude, nude, brutal, democratic—an apotheosis of femininity
placed within the reach of all; for the ballerines of the Eden dance
without *tutus,* and their beauty is revealed brutally without the
intervention of the light cloud of gauze that would render it more
desirable."[3]

Like Fanny Elssler, whose debut half a century before had
been preceded by a publicity stunt suggesting a liaison with the son
of Napoleon, Virginia appeared before the Paris audience in an aura
of a royal romance. Albert Wolff had revealed the story of her love
affair with the Count of Mirafiori in *Le Figaro* a few days before
her debut.[4] The publicity was so skilfully managed that the public
was filled with curiosity to see the new ballerina whose charms
had been so vividly described in the press.

At the moment of her first entrance the audience sensed,
with a peculiar thrill, that they were in the presence of an extraordinary talent. Every eye was on her as she stepped forward, a lovely
vision in a costume that revealingly showed off her physical attractions. The critic Panserose wrote of "a bust which she proudly displays in every aspect, a bust that is perfectly white with a light
pink make-up on the nipples, for Mlle. Zucchi hides nothing of her
nipples."[5] She was small, with a figure that was robust and elegant
and firm yet delicately shaped legs. Her face was framed by an un-
tamed mane of thick black hair which seemed to accentuate her
features and even give them a certain masculine look. Her complexion was, as one critic put it, "Italian, with sunshine under-
neath,"[6] and through it emerged a personality that was warm and
outgoing, with an appealing touch of childlike simplicity and artless charm. She was not pretty in the ordinary sense, but her features attracted by their mobility and expressiveness. One's first

impression of carnal charm was almost at once superseded by the
revelation of an extraordinary dramatic talent which "set her on a
level above the Cornalbas and the other teetotums."[7]

Her interpretation of the part of Sieba gripped the public
more and more as the action unfolded. In Sieba's first meeting
with the king she conveyed the overwhelming attraction he had
for her merely by the expression of her eyes, which she held firmly
fixed on him; and later, after their first kiss, there was none of the
conventional pressing of the heart and eye-rolling, but she simply
clasped her hands in joy like a young girl who has known no un-
happiness. But the most impressive demonstration of her acting
came in the Underworld scene. This was the highlight of the production. A spectacular colonnaded set stretched back the full
depth of the stage to where an ingenious arrangement of red and
blue gauzes simulated the effect of flames. A crowd of red-clad
demons and monsters filled the stage as Sieba was borne in by the
male dancers. After being dragged into the devilish round, she
broke free and found herself alone in the middle of the stage. Then,
in a remarkable passage of mime, her thoughts turned to the Paradise from which she had been expelled. She raised her arm slowly
towards Valhalla. At the thought of what she had lost her features
crumpled with despair. Tears streamed down her cheeks. She buried her face in her hands, and her shoulders shook with sobs. It
was the height of realism, and many eyes in the audience were wet
with tears.

In this brief scene she revealed herself, as Gustave Claudin
declared, to be "a tragedienne worthy of comparison with Rachel."[8]
It was, of course, touched with the spark of her own genius, but at
the same time it was a creation that was firmly founded on her
observation and experience. She had in fact drawn on a memory
from her early stage appearances, when her mother used to stand in
the wings with an expression of such unconcealed terror and anguish that the young dancer was quite overcome. "I had my

Virginia Zucchi at the age of seventeen. A photograph taken in Trieste in 1866. *(Museo di Storia ed Arte, Trieste)*

i in an unidentified role at the beginning of reer, c. 1869. *(Museo alla Scala, Milan)*

The dancer in an unidentified role played by her in the 1870s. *(Museo alla Scala, Milan)*

"The Fiasco of *Estella*, or a Star falls on Mont-Plaisir." A caricature by Oswald of
Ippolito Monplaisir's ballet *Estella*, in which Virginia Zucchi made her first appearance
at the Scala, Milan, in 1874. In the centre Raffaele Grassi and Virginia Zucchi are shown
in their *pas de deux. (Biblioteca Braidense, Milan)*

Scenes from Manzotti's ballet, *Rolla*, produced at the Scala, Milan, in 1876. Zucchi and Achille Coppini are depicted in their *pas de deux* at upper right. *(British Library, London)*

Virginia Zucchi as Tisbe in Pasquale Borri's *La Giocoliera* (Teatro Dal Verme, Milan, 1882). *(Museo alla Scala, Milan)*

As Civilisation in Manzotti's *Excelsior* (Scala, Milan 1883). *(Bakhrushin Theatre Museum, Moscow)*

Virginia Zucchi at the time of her Paris season, 1883. Photo: Reutlinger. *(Harvard Theatre Collection, Cambridge, Mass.)*

The underworld scene in Manzotti's *Sieba* at the Eden-Théâtre, Paris, in 1883, featuring Attilio Bonesi and Virginia Zucchi. Drawing by Adrian Marie. *(British Library, London)*

Virginia Zucchi in her valkyrie costume in *Sieba*
(Eden-Théâtre, Paris, 1883). Photo: Reutlinger.
(Harvard Theatre Collection, Cambridge, Mass.)

Georges Clairin's portait of Virginia Zucchi,
painted during her season at the Eden-
Théâtre, Paris, in 1883. *Musée de l'Opéra,
Paris)*

greatest success," she explained, "by imitating her in the scene in which Sieba is dragged unto the Underworld."[9]

Virginia's dancing created less sensation with an audience that had already seen the wonders of Cornalba's technique. Her first variation was in the spectacular fan tableau at the end of the banquet scene, when the back of the set divided to reveal an apotheosis of the female *corps de ballet* dressed in bejewelled costumes and forming an enormous animated fan. Virginia's variation, danced with a feather fan in her hand, was very original. It was a *pas de séduction* which she performed with great charm and grace, supported by a nimble male partner, Attilio Bonesi, and which contained a passage of *pointe* work travelling backwards which drew a murmur of astonishment from the audience.

Everyone was agog to meet the new celebrity who had burst upon the Paris scene. The journalist Marc de Valleyres managed to make her acquaintance and sensed how much of her own self went into her acting. He met her first on a bitterly cold December day, in the study of a literary friend. It was snowing outside, and he found her comfortably curled up in an armchair, warming her feet before the fire and sipping a glass of rum. On being introduced, she gave an embarrassed little smile and began playing with her hands like a little girl summoned before her teacher. When de Valleyres spoke of her performance, her expression, which till then had been languid and apathetic, became suddenly animated.

"What did you think of me?" she asked.

"A great artist," he murmured.

"Wouldn't I have made a great tragedienne?" she went on in a rather hard and rough tone of voice. "You have not seen me in *Brahma, Rolla* and *La Sorgente. I feel everything that I mime, believe me.*"

In another conversation de Valleyres thought he detected a hard streak in her character. He was telling how a certain young man had committed suicide—a story that perhaps struck a painful chord in Virginia's experience. She listened to him coldly, then, with a sudden flash of anger and vengeance, she cried: "Commit suicide for a man or woman—madness! People kill themselves because they have been unable to possess something, or because they have been betrayed, but then they die. It is very simple." Then her passion ebbed away, and she added with a smile, as if to reassure her listener: "But it is all play acting."

Was her anger sincere, de Valleyres wondered. He did not think so. He concluded that love had flown from her heart. But he saw that it had not left her untouched, for he was convinced that her "realistic and quasi-spoken miming" had its roots in the experience of her great love for Mirafiori, "From this almost pure passion," he concluded, "she has retained an absolute understanding in matters of love. Now she knows what she must believe, and certainly what she must hope for. Likewise, the dreams of yesterday have moulded her sighs and transports, her struggles and her abandon. On stage, as in real life, she can swoon, smile with moist quivering looks, blush with emotion and hide her head in her trembling hands, she can love and express it without in any way contaminating the memory of former kisses. To her first love Zucchi owes the authentic gestures and the thrilling sense of light and shade which make her, at all times and in all places, the perfect interpreter of love and modesty."[10]

She had taken a fifth-floor apartment in the Rue Godot de Mauroi, where she received friends and journalists amid a profusion of flowers and gave interviews in a rich Italian accent, speaking with complete candour of her private life. Did she have a protector? Marc de Valleyres suggested that she did. "Her way of living," he wrote, "is like that of any other actress. Two thousand francs a month cannot be enough for an elegant and ambitious woman. Félicien Champsaur made me laugh when, in a moment of enthusiastic admiration, he exclaimed: 'She lives off her art, simply and gloriously!' My first comment was 'What a good girl!' Then, when

I was told that she was like many others, my admiration switched
to Félicien. However, on reflection I believe that he knew those
little details, but he saw them with an eye that was benign and
veiled by love."[11]

Know them he did, as his writings were to show. Félicien
Champsaur, then a rising young journalist in his mid-twenties, was
one of Virginia's staunchest admirers and supporters. An obsession
with the *demi-monde* and back-stage gossip was to result in a series
of minor novels which have today been forgotten. But two of them
have a special interest in that they reveal his adoration of Virginia
Zucchi, of the beautiful woman as well as the incomparable dancer-
mime. To him she was one of the three women of the theatre—the
other two were Sarah Bernhardt and Thérésa, the popular singer—
who could "send a shiver of beauty quivering in the heads of those
who heard or saw them." In two of his books—*Miss América* (1885)
and *L'Amant des danseuses* (1888)—Virginia was portrayed, with
little attempt at concealment, as Eva Cordi.

In *Miss América* she makes only an incidental appearance,
but the book contains the most detailed description that has survived of her appearance in *Sieba* written by a young man una-
bashedly carried away by her physical attraction. He depicts her in
the opening scene, standing, in a beam of electric light, "a few
paces in front of the king, holding in her hands the divine sword
which she extends in a graceful gesture of offering, and gazing at
him lovingly with a long look of rapture. . . . Sieba cannot avert her
eyes from the object of her love. She looks at him with half-closed
eyes, as if in a dream. She seems to be absorbing the novel pleasure
which the sight of the young man has stirred in her, and to be savouring, cat-like, the unsuspected wonder which is pulsing through
her body. She glances down as though to retain the image of what
she has seen, but her joy produces a burning passion that stems
from the very heart of her being and passes with a voluptuous
glow through the thick black fringe of her lashes to envelop the

fair-haired king. Then suddenly she springs forward with an adorable little run and, presenting the sword, she instinctively and with a strange impulsive boldness presents her lips to those that she desires. She is about to touch them when, with a sudden recoil of her head of enchanting modesty, she exquisitely remembers herself.

"She runs off, and then returns, hardly seeming to touch the ground. These are not the academic pirouettes of a prima ballerina, thrown off with a banal stereotyped smile, but a dance that is almost winged, full of joy, supreme in its artistry, wondrously graceful, and given with a feeling that is original, profound and unexpectedly sensual. Overpowering and at times seemingly impromptu, it is the poetry of a sudden love.

"Her eyes, in turn bold, downcast, mischievous and inviting, flashing with a consuming flame—her rosy mouth, stirred for minutes on end by excitement—her hair, dark, uncontrolled, thick, making the whiteness of a gardenia burst out in its dark magic—her perfect shoulders, her elegant, rounded arms—her hands that attract, repel, implore, tremble, exult—her palpitating breasts—her complexion ablush with emotion—her tense huntress's legs, her thighs in which the blood is vibrant with desire—her whole body, venturesome or frightened, mimes incomparably the strophes of this song of tenderness, and in the intoxication of light and sound and frenzied bravos, there unfold chastity, longings, release, ecstasy, dreams and sudden awakenings.

"Splendid in her beauty and her nudity, bewitched, giving through the radiance of her flesh and the science of her heart such a direct sensation of her womanhood that the spectator can imagine himself to be her lover, she danced and acted the poem's prelude."[12]

In *L'Amant des danseuses* Champsaur elevated Virginia to become the heroine in a story of undisguised eroticism. The first part of the novel described an artist's passion for the ballerina—his

desire, his possession of her and his eventual disillusionment when
he discovers that she is unfaithful. The lurid details of the plot are
not relevant, but, by substituting Virginia's name for that of the
fictitious heroine, some of the descriptive passages reveal the extraordinary effect which she had on the impressionable young
writer.

"Every gesture, every look is instinct with passion. Her
entire being is as harmonious as an ode. Even when walking she reveals herself to be a dancer. She moves in a halo of voluptuousness,
of callipygean splendour—the heaving of her superb breasts, full and
firm, with their fascinating and dramatic motion, their curves oc-
casionally causing the dull pink tips to half emerge from the corsage; the flame of her red lips, moist and tender; the radiance of
her enormous eyes, black and deep, which stare, lure, fascinate
and inflame one's very bones; the irresistible appeal of her hands,
raised or clasped, or her white arms, her rounded shoulders, shaken
tragically by sobs when she is cast into the Underworld, or her
skin, her warm skin. She moves, powerfully and languidly, with a
lascivious roll of the hips. . . .

"With her the drama, poetic in its smallest details, whether
mimed or danced, takes flight. What an original talent! By turn
energetic, shy, angry, haughty, entreating, imploring, languid!
Expressions that are bewitching and magical! Her long black hair,
her long, thick, heavy hair, that magnificent pony's mane, what
splendour is there! What allure in its fragrant, pornaedic waves!
She is Salome, the assassin of John the Baptist; she is tempting,
enigmatic, corrupting, perverse, ingenuous, depraved, exquisite.
She subjugates men, haunts their imagination.

"Slender-waisted and supple, dressed only—in the marina-
resca scene—in blue net around the waist, on her flesh-coloured
tights, blue net that rises with the slightest eddy of her undulating
hips, her thighs uncovered, her legs firm and tensed, finely curved
and proud, almost nude—for she braves nudity, or at least the ap-

pearance of it, like Camargo, who was the first to wear a shortened skirt—[Virginia Zucchi], thrusting forward her chest or arching her lower back, to which from time to time she draws up the blue net, suddenly, after spinning dizzily round in her dance, falls back into the arms of the king with a quiver of kisses on her half-opened lips. Look now! On her mouth—what a genius, what a woman!—is there not a bouquet of desires!" [13]

And here, from the same book, is a more intimate portrait. "Sitting at her dressing-room table, cluttered with brushes and boxes, she looked into a triple mirror, quickly rouged her lips with a touch of a dampened, dark red pencil and powdered herself here and there with a little puff. She gave a few finishing touches to her stage face, and I saw in the mirror her eyes shining deep like wells of light. Finally she placed on her pretty head the silver helmet with two golden wings spreading out from the front, her valkyrie helmet, from which escapes her very long dark hair, with its spell of witchcraft—that prestigious fleece of night and beauty, alluring, entwining like a sheaf of vices and sins—her fascinating and perfumed hair which I, standing behind her, longed to take in my hands and kiss.

"We went down the stairs with La [Zucchi]. I looked at her again, from behind. Ah, her rump! I burned with the desire to spring at her, like a faun, to turn her round, to embrace her. What rapes, what crimes, dead as soon as born, flash through the minds of men, what thoughts are stifled or killed like mad dogs and obscene monkeys! It was a strange passion. Inwardly I fought the brutal frenzy of a cloven-footed satyr for this splendid dancer, whom I respect as one of those rare beings in whose soul some unknown power has distilled the elixir of magnetism, and whom I venerate as I would a poem." [14]

Few ballerinas can have exercised such a fascination as Virginia did during the few months she appeared in Paris. From the day of her debut there a growing cohort, elegant in their eve-

ning dress and sporting flowers in their button-holes, filled the
front rows of the stalls. At first these men were divided in their
loyalties, some championing the new star, and others supporting
Cornalba, who shared the role of Sieba with Virginia. It was not
long before Virginia, whose physical charms and dramatic genius
gave her an enormous advantage, won over nearly all the Cornal-
bists. Only the Comte de Cosnac remained loyal to her unfortunate
rival in the end. The Duc de Morny went over whole-heartedly to
the Zucchi camp; the Marquis de Caux was another admirer, as
were the painters Boldini and Clairin and a whole army of young
men about town who proudly exclaimed: "*Io sono zucchista!*"

The two ballerinas shared the role of Sieba throughout the
winter, Zucchi appearing 49 times and Cornalba 67 times.*
Virginia's last performance at the Eden was on March 14th, 1884,
and eight days later the ballet was taken off, after 121 consecutive
performances and a run of exactly four months.

In spite of the sensation she had caused, Virginia was not
to return to Paris until she was invited to stage the Venusberg
scene in *Tannhäuser* at the Opéra eleven years later. Did she leave
the French capital under a cloud, and was she really prevented
from returning by the fear of legal proceedings? That was the ex-
planation she was to give to a Russian journalist some years later.

In February 1884 the Spanish tenor, Julián Gayarre, made
his Paris debut at the Théâtre Italien as Gennaro in *Lucrezia
Borgia.* He was a man of splendid physique, with a voice that
thrilled the opera-going public. All Paris flocked to see and hear
him. Within a few days he had renewed his acquaintance with the
other celebrity of the town, Virginia Zucchi. The two found themselves passionately in love and became so engrossed with one another that they gave no thought to concealing their affair. Gayarre was
excessively possessive, while Virginia submitted herself completely

*Adele Besesti appeared in the role four times and Maria Saracco once.

to his demands. Even her most favoured admirers were suddenly forbidden to kiss her hand in her dressing-room. She became almost inaccessible, but even so Gayarre's suspicious could be aroused by the merest trifle.

There came an evening when he decided to put his mistress to the test. He burst into her dressing-room at the Eden-Théâtre during the interval after the first act of *Sieba*. Virginia was already in her costume for the second act.

In a state of great excitement he cried out: "Do you love me?"

"What a strange question!" Virginia replied, somewhat taken aback.

"Then are you ready to do anything for me?"

"Of course."

"Then come away from here."

"When?"

"This very minute."

Without saying another word Virginia threw a cloak over her costume and left the theatre with him.

The confusion that reigned after her sudden departure can be imagined. Such desertion in the course of a performance was unforgivable, and the management lost no time in bringing proceedings against the errant ballerina and obtaining judgment for a heavy sum in damages. To pay was quite beyond Virginia's means, and for some years she dared not set foot in Paris for fear of judicial consequences.

This story has to be accepted on Virginia's word alone, for the proceedings were apparently not reported, possibly because they were settled before coming before a court. There is, however, circumstantial evidence of Gayarre's occasional presence at the Eden, for only a few days before her last performance there he was reported to be concerned in a project to form a new opera company which was to be based both in London and in Paris, at the Eden.

Virginia was unusually candid about her affairs of the heart, and it
is such details which experienced reporters endeavour to extract
to give spice to their stories. She also knew their value in relation
to publicity, and in the interview she gave to the Russian journalist
in 1889, this incident had a bearing on her interpretation in
Esmeralda, which had just been seen in St. Petersburg. "Mlle.
Zucchi," the journalist concluded, "is positively made for this
role. She is able to love and is always ready to sacrifice everything
to the man she loves."[15]

Professionally the remaining months of 1884 were a fallow
period. Her affair with Gayarre and then the death, in July, of her
father kept her from the stage until the end of the year, when she
accepted an engagement at the Teatro Regio, Turin, for Carnival
1884–85. There, fully refreshed, she threw herself into her work
with renewed vigour and a new-found resolution. She had two
important new roles to learn. The first was in *Rodope*, a new ballet
by a young choreographer, Raffaele Grassi, in which she played
the Thracian slave girl Rodope, who falls in love with Aesop and
swears revenge when he prefers freedom without her to remaining
with her in bondage. It contained a highly charged mime scene at
the point where Aesop has made his fateful choice. In an instant
Rodope is transformed from a young girl in love into a woman
consumed with bitter hatred. She reproaches Aesop with his treach-
ery and threatens him with a terrible vengeance. Then, as if already
set on her future career as a courtesan, she turns to the elderly
merchant Iadmon, ready to accept his caresses without revulsion.
It was a scene that fitted Virginia's dramatic style perfectly, and it
was a pity that the ballet, which became quite popular in Italy for
some years, was never afterwards revived with her in the role she
had created. The other part which the Regio had ready for her was
one that would remain in her repertory until the end of her career
and in fact be the role in which she would make her last appearance on the stage—the ebullient Swanilda in *Coppélia*.

During this season in Turin, a city that held many memories for her, she had put her talents and her stamina to a stern test. She now looked forward to a novel experience that was to occupy the summer months—a visit to distant St. Petersburg. She saw it, no doubt, only as a pleasant interlude of no special significance, from which she would return to resume her career where she had left off.

Kin Grust

As the train carried her comfortably towards St. Petersburg, Virginia's thoughts might understandably have turned more frequently to the fabled glories of the city that awaited her at the end of her journey, the capital of the Tsars with its elegant architecture and its white nights, than to her professional commitment there. For her engagement was for only a few weeks, in a popular pleasure garden on the city's outskirts, and at a very modest fee. She could not have suspected what a historic turning point her visit would be: that it was to set a seal of imperishable glory on her career and even to have the most far-reaching consequences on the development of ballet.

The initial impulse which had led to her journey to Russia had come from the theatre critic, Constantin Apollonovich Skalkovsky, who wrote on ballet for the paper *Novoye Vremya* under the pseudonym "Balletomane." During a stay in Milan a few years before he had been urged to see her by the singer Virginia Ferni-Germano and had fallen under the spell of her genius at first sight. On his return to Russia he wrote about her dancing in an article on Milan, and in his book *Ballet, Its History and Place among the Elegant Arts*, published in 1882, he listed the finest contemporary ballerinas as "Flindt, Cornalba, and particularly Virginia Zucchi."[1] It was the glowing reference in his article, he claimed, that prompted Mikhail Valentinovich Lentovsky, the lessee of the Livadia Gardens in St. Petersburg, to engage Virginia to appear at the head of a small ballet company in an extravaganza.

Lentovsky, whom Skalkovsky was to acclaim as "the saviour of our ballet"[2] for his perspicacity in importing Virginia Zucchi to Russia, was in the prime of his manhood when their paths crossed. His enormous strength and his abundant energy must have made an immediate impression on her. Black-bearded and broad-shouldered, and sporting a long-waisted *poddyovka,* with medals pinned at his chest, a silk shirt and high lacquered boots, he cut an impressive figure as he walked about his pleasure gardens invariably attended by a following of friends and hangers-on. He had begun as an actor on the Moscow stage and in 1878 had taken over the Hermitage Gardens which, under his management, acquired a reputation both for respectability and for the quality of its entertainments. He had now come to St. Petersburg to apply this formula for success to the Livadia Gardens, which had been renamed Kin Grust, or Abandon Sorrow.

During the summer months court and society were wont to leave St. Petersburg to the humbler and less fortunate of its citizens. The Imperial Theatres closed their doors, and many of those who remained in the city sought amusement in the pleasure gardens and summer theatres on the Islands. Kin Grust was one of these, situated only a short steamer journey from the centre of the city. Lentovsky, who spent money with careless freedom, had transformed the old Livadia out of all recognition. The theatre, which many people could remember as a hay barn, had been enlarged and redecorated in the old Russian manner, and given a new proscenium in the Pompeian style. The surrounding gardens were filled with many other attractions: Moorish kiosks and a vast Kirghiz tent, where Lentovsky and his cronies were usually to be found quaffing his favourite Benedictine, a refreshment room in the Chinese style and a spacious Italianate verandah running along the river, green lawns, a winter garden heavy with the scents of tropical plants and, in front of the theatre itself, a tall column surmounted by a figure of Mercury bearing a torch that shone with the steady brilliance of electric light.

To gardens such as these people of all classes came in large numbers in the light summer evenings, packing the buffets—it was said that the success of the enterprise depended on the number of sandwiches consumed—and savouring the distractions that seemed to start all at once at the sound of a bell. "Attendants sprang into action, gymnasts turned somersaults, Abdul Kerim walked on the tight-rope balancing on his head a steaming samovar and a complete tea service, actors performed a vaudeville. Darkness had fallen, the electric lights were turned on, and on the Neva the skiffs were moored in line with lamps at their prows. It was really a beautiful sight."[3] Then the bell rang again to announce that the performance in the theatre was about to begin.

It was on such a signal, on the evening of June 18th, 1885, that the curtain rose on Offenbach's operetta, *Le Voyage dans la lune.* No expense, it seemed, had been spared. The production had cost nearly 40,000 roubles, most of which had been spent on the scenery and costumes, which had been purchased from the Alhambra in London. No less than two hundred and forty-five persons had been assembled to take part, and a distinguished ballet-master, Joseph Hansen, who had worked for a few years for the Imperial Theatres in Moscow, had been engaged to produce the two incidental ballets: the Ballet of the Stars in Act II and the Ballet of Swallows and Snow in Act III. As the musicians took their places for the overture, the theatre was filled to overflowing, with many spectators crowding the passage-ways. The new operetta was a strong attraction in itself, but many spectators had come out of curiosity to see Virginia Zucchi, for it was nearly twenty years since an Italian ballerina had been seen in St. Petersburg.

There was no denying that Virginia was making her Russian debut under distinctly unfavourable circumstances. She appeared only briefly in the course of a lengthy performance, the stage was small with poorly carpentered boards that were not even damped, the view of the spectators in the front seats was impeded by the raised footlights, she lacked the support of a male partner,

and—as a final indignity—she had caught a heavy cold on arriving
in St. Petersburg. Yet in spite of all this she succeeded in imposing
herself at once as a ballerina of remarkable and original gifts. The
critic Alexandre Pleshcheyev retained a vivid impression of her in
the variation in the first ballet which she danced entirely on the
pointes to a well-known waltz song by K. S. Shilovsky called "Do
You Remember?" She was costumed, he remembered, in white,
carrying a nosegay of flowers, her wavy hair falling loose on her
shoulders. Analysing the impression she made on him, he concluded that her secret lay not in the perfect proportions of her
figure, nor the expressiveness of her features, nor even her *pointes,*
but in the way she held her hands, "their plastic quality, their fluidity and their natural grace," and the compelling power of her
eyes which "even under the illumination of the electric spot-light
transpierced the audience."[4] Her friend Skalkovsky was delighted
to observe the warmth of her reception at her first entrance—a
rare honour for a debutante—and the attentiveness of the audience
when she began to dance. Her reception at the beginning of the
second ballet reached the proportions of an ovation, and she was
presented with a large basket of flowers. In this second ballet she
was able to give a hint—it could be little more—of her dramatic
talent, when she portrayed a swallow which is found freezing in
the snow and is gradually restored to life. Her triumph was not in
doubt, and the Italian ambassador, Count Greppi, who was an assiduous theatre-goer, elegantly complimented her on gaining a
complete victory on the banks of the Neva.

    In *Novoye Vremya* two days later Skalkovsky wrote of her
qualities in phrases that were to be long remembered and often
quoted. "At a time when plastic ballerinas are usually heavy and
lumbering, and aerial ballerinas look like spiders and can seldom
cope with their long hands, Mlle. Zucchi offers a remarkable
balance of all the choreographic qualities. There is elegance in her
entire figure, and her head, crowned by hair that is frequently

tousled, is enlivened by eyes which at need assume a wonderful passionate expression. Her miming, therefore, stems not from her eyes alone, but from her whole body, which is marvellously proportioned. At a time when the majority of ballerinas have legs which are developed to the detriment of other parts of the body, Mlle. Zucchi, who possesses the legs of Diana, has also delicate hands of utter beauty, perfect shoulders, a well-formed bust and a spine in which there is more poetry than in half the contemporary Italian poets put together."[5]

Kin Grust was, of course, a far cry from the conventional elegance of the Imperial stage. The *corps de ballet* was a hastily assembled company of dancers from Milan and Vienna who lacked the discipline and uniform training of the St. Petersburg Theatre School. Also they were costumed in a style that was very foreign to Russian eyes, with short ballet skirts in the Italian fashion, and sometimes in tights that revealed the whole form of the legs. The effect of this daring display was revealed in a satirical paragraph in the *Peterburgskaya Gazeta,* recording the description given to his wife by a merchant returning home rather drunk from a visit to Kin Grust. "Zucca," he tells her in a thick voice, "dances in a petticoat, but all the other mademoiselles dance without even that. . . just like acrobats."[6]

As her fame spread, there were people who viewed her arrival with displeasure, for her appearance marked the first real breach of the monopoly which the Imperial Theatres had long enjoyed in the realm of ballet. This monopoly had been formally abolished three years before, but until Lentovsky's enterprise at Kin Grust, no private impresario had ventured to present ballet in competition with the lavishly subsidised Bolshoi Theatre. Now that a foreign ballerina had actually appeared, the champions of the old order scented danger. Some of these, looking for weaknesses and refusing to acknowledge her merits, criticised her for lacking elevation, and several dancers of the Imperial Theatres who made

their way to Kin Grust went away grumbling that she was a poor
dancer.

But others viewed her more impartially. V.N., in *Teatralny
Mirok,* noted her special qualities as "an inborn grace and elasticity.
Her whole figure is elegant, and her movements gentle and smooth.
When she dances, she is not only dancing but acting as well. . . .
With most ballerinas one can see how they conceal what in balletic
language is called force, but with Mlle. Zucchi all her movements
and steps lead into one another without the slightest effort. In
matters of technique. . . Mlle. Zucchi does not perform any special
difficulties, but the *double rond de jambe* and in particular her
pointes, from which she does not descend throughout one whole
dance, attracted the attention of the connoisseurs of the art of
ballet."[7]

That summer Alexandre Benois, a boy of fifteen, was
living in St. Petersburg with his parents. He was already a devotee
of the ballet, and among his treasures was an engraving of Virginia
Zucchi which he had cut out from the weekly magazine *Niva* the
year before. Nobody in his family could tell him about this fascinating creature and, when he learnt one day that she was actually
in St. Petersburg and appearing at Kin Grust, he and an English
friend slipped away to see her. It was a warm June evening, and
they went to the Islands by steamer. When writing his memoirs, he
recalled that there were many empty seats in the theatre, a statement that conflicts with the newspaper reports of full houses,
which were no doubt inserted by the Kin Grust management.

Zucchi's appearance in the first ballet lasted no more than
ten minutes, but as Benois recalled, "those ten minutes were a
revelation to me. The ecstasy of delight that I experienced caused
an utter revolution in my outlook on dancing and brought it into
line with the ideal which was taking shape in my subconscious
mind. The ballet had nothing in common with the rest of the ope-

retta. It was just a choreographic number, devoid of subject or drama. I am laying special stress on this point as later on Virginia Zucchi aroused the wildest enthusiasm of the Russian public by the dramatic intensity of her miming. On this early occasion, even the small audience seated here and there in the stalls and boxes seemed instantly to appreciate Zucchi's appearance on the stage and showed this by the breathless intentness with which they watched her. Towards the end of her dance she rose on her points and, taking tiny steps, began gliding backwards to the music of a very popular song, *Nur für Natur*—it seemed as though she were being wafted by a gentle breeze. At first there were individual bursts of applause, but soon the whole audience broke out into a stormy ovation. Zucchi was forced to give two encores. Even then the public was not satisfied and remained in the empty, barn-like theatre applauding and shouting the name that was shortly to be on everybody's lips."[8]

The impact of Zucchi's artistry was so strong that the boy returned to Kin Grust whenever he had an opportunity before he had to leave St. Petersburg to stay with his sister in Kharkov. The news of the extraordinary ballerina was spreading fast, and on each visit the theatre was noticeably fuller. The enthusiastic support of a band of balletomanes, who even at this early stage recognised the importance of securing her services for the Imperial Theatres, was having its effect. No task was too menial for them, as Skalkovsky, who was one of them, explained. "One copied music for her, a second saw she was well known at court, a third moved scenery at rehearsals, a fourth fetched water for her, a fifth initiated the public through the newspapers into the mysteries of the 'Divine One's' forthcoming work, a sixth induced the ballerina to wash her hands with soap almost for the first time in her life, and so on—and in the end a colossal success was achieved."[9] As a final seal on her renown Raoul Gunsbourg impersonated her at the Arcadia summer theatre,

giving such a neat imitation of her spinning round the stage on her
pointes that the comedian Joseph Roux exclaimed: "*Ce n'est pas
Zucchi, c'est Zucchi le fils!*"

Skalkovsky became a devoted friend. The character of the
ballerina fascinated him, for she was so utterly different from the
type to which a theatrical star was supposed to conform. He discovered, for instance, that she was very miserly by nature and,
paying her a visit in the *dacha* where she was staying, he was surprised to observe how parsimoniously she lived. Seeing her wash
her hands in juice pressed from lemons, he brought her a present
next day of a bar of soap, which she proceeded to divide with a
thread into three parts, saying: "One for me, one for my brother
Vittorio and the third for my sister Costantina." A few days later
she allowed him to give her a small box of tooth powder which
she carefully wrapped up in paper and put into her pocket. She
seemed quite oblivious of her appearance: she chewed her nails,
she tidied her hair by running her fingers through it and she made
no pretence at being elegant. One day at the end of June he met
her walking in Kin Grust, wearing a tattered squirrel-fur coat. She
was brimming over with enthusiasm.

"I adore your country life," she exclaimed.

"But where have you seen it?" he asked, puzzled.

"Here in Novaya Derevnya," she replied innocently, refer-
ring to a neighbouring suburb as if it were in the very depths of
the countryside.

He was delighted by her spontaneity. Although to him she
was only semi-literate and seemed not to have read anything at all,
he realised that she was extraordinarily clever and was capable of
making sound judgments. He listened to her for hours as she talked
and gesticulated over a glass of red wine, and the better he knew
her, the more his amusement at her eccentricities turned into a
genuine admiration. He appreciated her natural aesthetic taste
which he found no less stimulating than the inborn grace of her

movements, and he was constantly amazed at her unquenchable store of energy. "Where there's will, there's a way" was her watchword.

Seldom had he come across a more original character. She always arrived at the theatre clutching a large bag which contained, among other things, a collection of odd pieces of iron that she had picked up for luck and a bottle filled with what she assured Skalkovsky was an elixir given to her by her mother. One day he took an opportunity to sniff this precious liquid, which he discovered to be nothing more than ordinary vodka. This bottle held poignant memories for her, and once he found her in tears before it. What was the matter, he asked. She had lost her mother, she replied. When did this happen, he enquired in a tone of concern. Seven years ago, she sobbed.[10]

For a divinity she was surprisingly down-to-earth. "Virginia," Skalkovsky said rather plaintively, "possesses much poetry, but two days ago I sent her twelve bottles of wine and today some twenty bottles. On the stage poetry, but at home too much prose. With my wine she regales her compatriots, the macaroni-eaters, who are living in Petersburg."[11]

A month after Virginia's debut at Kin Grust, on July 21st, Lentovsky presented his second production—Edmond Audran's operetta *Les Pommes d'or*, featuring, in addition to her, another Italian ballerina, Maria Giuri, an enlarged *corps de ballet* of "young women wearing as little as possible,"[12] and Charles Lauri, the English pantomimist, in the role of the marmozet. Giuri had been prima ballerina in Warsaw and London and had the unique honour of having appeared before the Emperors of Germany, Austria and Russia when they met at Czernowitz in 1884. Virginia was only stimulated to greater efforts, and to her admirers' delight she established her supremacy with seemingly effortless ease in the inserted ballet, which was judged the most interesting element in an otherwise nonsensical work. It was a ballet of games, beginning with those of childhood, and culminating with baccarat, roulette and love games. These love games, wrote Skalkovsky, Virginia was able to portray with great conviction because, as he observed, "her manner of dancing is as elegantly erotic as the verses of Ovid or de Musset."[13] Costumed in black, she performed a Spanish dance, a variation in waltz time on her *pointes* and two galops, revealing "lightness, grace and assurance, and that supreme art which consists in the ability to conceal difficulties. Mlle. Zucchi danced as if for the sheer pleasure and enjoyment of it."[14] It was noticed, too, that she was dancing with exceptional fire, inspired, it was suggested, by the abandon of some gypsy dancers she had seen at Arcadia a few days before.

Lentovsky's next production was *The Forest Vagabond*, in which she was called upon to dance at short notice and without any rehearsals. For this she chose from her repertory a character dance with a carbine which she performed impeccably in a "cunningly revealing" costume.[15]

It was becoming increasingly apparent that despite the enormous receipts, to which Zucchi contributed in no small measure, Lentovsky's enterprise was not prospering. Having engaged her for only a few weeks, he had persuaded her to prolong her stay at three times her original salary. But not even she could turn failure into success. Half way through the season Lentovsky was forced by insolvency to withdraw, and for the remaining weeks of the summer the theatre remained open through the initiative of the artists themselves. During August Virginia danced at Kin Grust without remuneration so as to help her less fortunate colleagues. And finding herself in a position to dictate the programme—and, as Skalkovsky disclosed, "wishing finally to kill off her rival," Giuri[16]—she decided to stage a curtailed version of *Brahma*, which was first given on August 15th at a benefit performance in aid of the administration.

Until now she had given St. Petersburg no more than a hint of her dramatic talent, but now she prepared to reveal the full extent of her histrionic genius. It was a bold undertaking. Hansen had left, and she had to shoulder the full responsibility of producing the ballet at the barest minimum of expense, with only a week of rehearsals, and with a small, mediocre company that had to be augmented by the Lauri-Lauri troupe of English pantomimists. A cast of about eighty was needed to do justice to the ballet, and there was barely a quarter of that number at her disposal. There were no male dancers in the company, and this lack had to be filled by the pantomimists. They were very willing, but communication was difficult because the clowns spoke only English, of which Virginia knew not a word. And when she did get her message across to them, there was a wide divergence between their style and the style of mime which the ballet demanded. "Imagine you are bored," she told them at one point, a command they obeyed by standing stock still, indulging in enormous yawns. The score had to be hurriedly reorchestrated from a piano reduction for the sparse band of musicians—a task no doubt performed by one of her devoted balletomanes—and the scenery and costumes had to be selected from what was available, with such surprising but unavoidable results as the use of a set representing a Rhineland landscape for an Indian scene!

It was also necessary to simplify the ballet, which was reduced to four scenes. In the process Virginia made a significant change in the plot by introducing another character, Kalia, a companion to Padmana. In the absence of printed scenarios the motive for the attempt to kill Brahma had to be explained clearly, and Virginia's solution was to have Kalia, in a fit of jealousy, hire assassins to perform the deed. An even more radical change followed in the last scene, which was adapted from another ballet by Monplaisir, *Le Figlie di Cheope.* Although it is Padmana who has saved his life, Brahma returns to the arms of Kalia. Padmana stabs herself in despair, and the last few minutes of the ballet, when the dying Padmana is torn between hatred and love, cursing and forgiving Brahma and her rival in turn, and finally expires in the arms of her companions, provided Virginia with the opportunity of an impressive display of histrionics.

It was during August that young Alexandre Benois returned to St. Petersburg. He was so eager to see Virginia again that he rushed to Livadia on the very evening of his arrival. To his surprise there were no tickets available at the box office, and he could only get in by paying a tout three times the normal price. His youthful impressions of *Brahma* remained with him to the end of his long life.

"The performance", he recalled, "did not consist of the whole of Monplaisir's ballet but of several fragments. Only one of these has remained in my memory—the one that attracted the public and brought forth the wildest enthusiasm. This fragment showed the flight of the Bayadère (again a Bayadère!) and her lover Brahma from their enemies and the halt of the fugitives in a tropical forest. The scenery demanded a great deal of imagination from the audience, as the stage was ill-lit and what was visible was much more like a stunted St. Petersburg public square than a luxuriant tropical jungle. The lovers were discovered, faint and tired and hardly able to drag their feet along, peering with horror into the surrounding gloom and approaching a cardboard rock, on which Brahma sank down exhausted. Suddenly a band of bearded, white-clad men emerged from the darkness and crept towards the sleepers. But Zucchi the Bayadère was wide awake. From that moment onwards, thanks to the spotlight—electric sun, as it was then called—every change of expression on her mobile face could be seen. She kissed lovingly the forehead of her prince. Lying by his side she first only senses and then, still feigning sleep, actually watches the approach of danger. Zucchi's change of expression was so marvellously beautiful that these few seconds alone were worth the whole ballet. The conspirators surround their victims and, pulling out their daggers, raise them, and are just about to plunge them into the sleeping

prince when an extraordinary thing happens. The feeble, unarmed
girl who, but a few moments ago, could hardly walk, rises suddenly
to her feet and begins to advance towards the would-be murderers,
holding them with her eyes. It is impossible to describe this moment. The scene when related is apt to appear as ridiculous as any
melodramatic nonsense. But those who saw Zucchi could not have
laughed. There was such pathos, such supreme self-sacrifice, such
feminine fury in the woman fighting for the life of her beloved,
and finally, such tremendous magnetic force! The play demanded
that the plotters should withdraw, forced by the magic force of
Padmana's eyes, and indeed it was obvious that they were not simply following the producer's directions, but were actually compelled to do so by Zucchi's piercing gaze.

"My brother Louis corroborated this impression when,
several months later, he told me about the following incident. At
a dinner party given by the balletomane I. I. Rostovtsev in honour
of Zucchi, it was decided to perform that scene to my brother
Albert's improvisations on the piano. Dinner napkins were quickly
transformed into turbans on the heads of the amateur actors, the
prince turned his frock-coat inside out, and Zucchi ruffled the
mass of her raven black hair and only slightly tucked up her evening dress. A couch served as the rock and two or three tropical
plants in pots became the forest. In spite of these surroundings,
the scene was performed so convincingly that, after it was over,
my brother felt as though his eyes had been blinded by some brilliant light. . . .

"How perfectly adorable Zucchi became after her victory,
when, radiant with joy, she awakened her sleeping lover and insisted on continuing their journey! There was such genuine love in
her eyes, such joy in every movement, such simplicity and unaffected charm in her whole personality. How worthy of love she
seemed and how one hoped and wished that this happiness would

not forsake her! The whole audience, which had just been trembling for her, now heaved a sigh of relief and relaxed, believing that
she would be saved."[17]

Her performance of the daggers scene attained such a pitch
of realism that many spectators were reduced to tears, and on one
occasion two ladies were so affected that they had to be carried
out in a faint.

Virginia's magic now held St. Petersburg in thrall. Skalkovsky compared her dramatic gifts with those of the great Italian tragedienne Adelaide Ristori. Pleshcheyev thought that Fanny Elssler
and Carolina Rosati might have equalled her in the dramatic line,
but, as he pointed out, that was so long ago that only Arcady
Pokhvisnev, who called himself "the oldest balletomane," could
make a valid comparison. The question was soon settled by the old
connoisseur himself when he categorically declared, with the ardent
enthusiasm of a youth in love: "We have lived to see a second
Elssler!"[18]

As a dancer, too, Virginia was commanding increasing respect. "What fascinated us above everything else," wrote the critic
V.P. in the *Journal de St. Pétersbourg,* after seeing her in *Brahma,*
"was the delicacy and rhythmical musicality of her steps, the
voluptuously abandoned yet graceful movements, and her gaiety
and recklessness which every now and then break out, even if she
does not attain the speed of some of her celebrated predecessors.
One can see that she is an extraordinary ballerina who can be criticised only for the, so to speak, acrobatic nature of her dancing—
this is a defect of the contemporary school—and a certain lack of
elegance, a fault which will quickly disappear on contact with the
splendours of our Imperial stage if, as we are assured, she is really
engaged there." [19]

At the time this was no more than an inspired prophesy,
but such was the extent of her triumph at Kin Grust that it could
only be a matter of time before an offer would be made by the

Imperial Theatres. With this prospect in mind, she refused several
lucrative offers during the summer. Meanwhile much discussion
and argument went on behind closed doors in the office of the
Imperial Theatres. In the past it had long been customary to engage leading ballerinas from abroad, but since the departure of
Adele Grantzow in 1873 the Imperial Theatres had relied exclusively on native talent. Recently, however, Ivan Vsevolozhsky, the Director of the Imperial Theatres, had been very concerned about the
poor attendance at ballet performances, and this crisis of popularity
had been heightened by the retirement of Ekaterina Vazem and the
imminent departure of Maria Gorshenkova. With only one ballerina remaining, Vsevolozhsky foresaw difficulties in presenting three
ballet performances a week, and in a report to the Minister he suggested that the remedy was to invite a distinguished ballerina from
the West as guest artist. His superiors were apparently not convinced, although enquiries, which came to nothing, seem to have
been made to ascertain if Rosita Mauri and Elena Cornalba were
available. So the ballet of the Imperial Theatres had continued
along its time-honoured course, so hide-bound in its conservatism
that no movement for progress or reform rose even within its own
ranks.

When Italian-trained ballerinas—first Zucchi, then Maria
Giuri and Albertina Flindt—began to appear on private stages in St.
Petersburg in 1885, the situation changed dramatically. The excitement which Virginia caused involved the balletomanes and the general public, and demands that she be engaged at the Imperial Theatres grew more insistent with each passing week. Vsevolozhsky may
not have changed his mind about the need to inject foreign talent
into the Imperial company, but he was doubtful whether Virginia
Zucchi, with her very individual talent, would fit into the type of
productions that were staged at the Bolshoi. His ballet-master,
Marius Petipa, shared his doubts, considering her to be "undisci-
plined" and scorning her, unjustly, for having been unable to ob-

tain an engagement at the Paris Opéra: with Sangalli and Mauri in possession there, there had never been any question of that. When the extent of Virginia's triumph gave cause for alarm, it was defensively suggested that it would be better to invite Giuri instead, even though she had earlier been considered unsuitable for the Imperial stage.

Such was the state of confusion in which the authorities found themselves when Virginia was commanded to appear at the Imperial summer theatre at Krasnoye Selo before the Imperial family and the court. The invitation was delivered only three days before the performance, so there was no time to prepare anything special, and she decided to appear in a few excerpts from *Le Voyage dans la lune*, which were adapted to include parts for two male dancers from the Imperial Theatres, Lev Ivanov and Sergei Litavkin.* Her first real contact with Russian dancers brought mixed impressions. Ivanov's experienced advice and courtesy made a pleasing impression on her, and her young partner Litavkin inspired her with the confidence she needed to overcome the coldness shown to her by the other dancers taking part.

When the great day arrived Skalkovsky escorted her to the theatre. On the way she suddenly ordered the driver to stop. She leapt out of the *drozhsky* and grabbed a large handful of hay from a passing cart, which she stuffed into her capacious handbag. "This is probably going to bring me luck," she announced to her surprised companion, and they continued happily on their way.

A few hours later, when the performance began, her exuberance had subsided. She began to feel conscious of the comparison that would be made between herself, a woman of thirty-six, and the Russian ballerinas who not only had the advantage of youth, but had just returned fresh and in full strength from their

---

*Sergei Spiridovich Litavkin, father of the Sergei Litavkin (1891–1915) who partnered Adeline Genée.

summer holidays. Exhausted though she was from appearing nightly at Kin Grust, she passed this test with flying colours and won
many more admirers in the circles of influence. She was greeted
with storms of applause, and was made to repeat her variation to
"Do You Remember?" the melody of which, played by a first-
rate orchestra, sounded more haunting than ever.

It was perhaps of this performance that a contemporary
critic wrote that *"when Zucchi waltzes, she waltzes passion. The
music seems to be pouring its sweet poison into the black-haired
Italian; her whole being trembles to the slightest tempo of the orchestra. Her glance, her smile, the tossing back of her dishevelled
tresses, all are done to time; even her legs, hands, shoulders, neck—
can one say more?—flow with the music; and then suddenly there
is a broad flight, a long leap, a whirlwind, and the exhilarated girl
is caught in the arms of her cavalier like some flying apparition in
a bacchanale."*[20]

Later in August she enjoyed another triumph at Pavlovsk,
where the demand to see her in *Brahma* far exceeded the number
of seats available.

Now that she had danced before the Tsar and clearly
pleased him, the decision to engage her at the Imperial Theatres
could be delayed no longer. A last-minute rearguard action by the
critic and balletomane D. D. Korovyakov was of no avail. Korovyakov took for his line of attack a lack of good schooling which he
found in her inability to control the ardour of her temperament.
Surprisingly he cited as an example the daggers scene in *Brahma*,
accusing her of exaggeration in her movements and gestures and
of the use of artificial devices, such as "gliding across the stage,
like a ghost in a tragedy" as she advanced on the assassins with her
imperious gesture. He detected the same lack of schooling in her
dancing, citing a tendency towards acrobatics, a lack of elevation
and an angular sharpness in some of her movements in allegro.
These faults he linked with the type of ballet-faery which was be-

coming popular in Western Europe, but Skalkovsky was quick to point out that Virginia had made her name in important dramatic ballets. In conclusion Korovyakov attributed her extraordinary success in St. Petersburg to the coarse and sensual taste of the uninitiated masses who frequented the pleasure gardens.

Korovyakov's outburst did her little harm. Public opinion was unmistakably showing itself. Petipa was seen as the main obstacle. A writer in *Teatralny Mirok* asked: "What does it matter if Virginia Zucchi does not find favour with the ballet-master?" "Surely the engagement of the beautiful artist cannot depend on him? The best society, so to speak, of St. Petersburg is united in its enthusiasm for her, and suddenly, because of some intangible shortcoming and perhaps just competitive fault-finding, it is deprived of the pleasure of seeing her regularly. . . . Audiences at the Bolshoi Theatre grow more sparse every day and every year, and only a mighty talent such as hers can take us back to the glorious past and preserve the fragments of the unforgettable traditions of the leading ballet stage."[21]

In the face of this growing demand Vsevolozhsky and Petipa were forced to reconsider their attitude.

There was also considerable opposition within the company to take into account. It was argued that the dancers belonging permanently to the Imperial Theatres had the sole right to appear on the Imperial stage on the ground that they were prohibited from accepting engagements elsewhere—a proposition that was weakened by the fact that a number of them had danced on other stages without objection. At one time feelings in the company ran so high that the management felt obliged to justify its new stance by emphasising that Virginia was an artist from the Scala, Milan, and alleging that she had found herself at Kin Grust through a misunderstanding of its importance. There was some talk of strike action if she were to be engaged, but in the end it proved to be "a storm in a tea-cup which quickly subsided" when it was realised that the decision was now final. [22]

In the change of attitude that took place in the company, a significant role was played by Varvara Nikitina, who had gone to Kin Grust several times to see Virginia dance. The two ballerinas may have discovered a bond between them, for Virginia, on her arrival in St. Petersburg, stayed in the same *dacha* which had been Nikitina's home two years before. Nikitina had the courage to declare herself in favour of inviting Virginia to the Imperial stage, and some of the more intelligent dancers withdrew their opposition and began to study her technique and see what lessons were to be learnt. Thus, by the end of the summer the matter was settled. On September 4th, amid wild scenes, with admirers clambering on to the stage to celebrate her triumph with her, Virginia gave her final performance, for her own benefit, at Kin Grust. Earlier that day Vsevolozhsky had invited her to his office to sign the contract with the Imperial Theatres, but as she was about to put pen to paper she was seized with a sudden thought. "On a Friday, never!" she said firmly. Nothing would move her, and the signing had to be deferred to the following day. The "divine one" then departed for Milan, not only taking memories of the warmth of the Russian public but ruefully thinking of all the roubles that Lentovsky had failed to pay her. Lentovsky, who was a sensitive man, was contrite and crestfallen. He freely admitted that he had overstretched his resources by re-engaging her on such lavish terms. Making a play on the title, *Vain Precautions*, which the Russians give to *La Fille mal gardée*, he remarked wryly that it had been a little matter of vain proportions.

The Imperial Stage:
Aspiccia and Lise

Virginia Zucchi's first contract with the Imperial Theatres was for sixteen performances between December 13th, 1885 and March 13th, 1886. For this she was to receive a total of 6,000 roubles and the proceeds of a benefit performance. The management was to supply the costumes and character head-dresses for the ballets, while she for her part was to provide "tights and camisoles as well as ordinary head-dresses, and the shoes which her roles required." She was to be in St. Petersburg by November 27th, so as to allow time for the rehearsals needed to fit her into the ballet that was being prepared for her debut.[1]

It was understood that this was to be *La Fille mal gardée*, which she knew well in the version that Paul Taglioni had arranged to the music of Hertel. This ballet had been performed at intervals in St. Petersburg since early in the century, and the sensation which Fanny Elssler had created in the role of Lise was still a cherished memory for some of the older balletomanes. It was now many years since it had been given in St. Petersburg, and it was decided that Petipa should prepare a new production, using Hertel's music. The obliging Skalkovsky was asked to write to the ballerina about obtaining the music.

She replied from Como on October 10th: "My dear friend, I certainly see that you are all very worried about me. The cause of it was a little journey to Italy which I have just made. The music of *La Fille mal gardée* can be obtained, but for 400 marks, and as I have no wish to pay this out of my own pocket, I do not know if I can get it in Italy. I must thank you for the telegram you sent me, only do not think I was taken in by your little joke—that the management had asked you to write and tell me they were displeased with me—and be assured that as soon as I have arranged something regarding the music I will hasten to let you know who has the rights. Nevertheless, as I want to be present at the rehearsals, there is no need for it to reach you as early as that. I still think back, dear friend, to the excellent reception I was given in the country that is the coldest in Europe, but in its love of art the warmest, and I assure you that I shall be enchanted the day I arrive in St. Petersburg."[2]

Meanwhile the season had opened at the Bolshoi Theatre with a performance of *Le Diable à quatre* that had aroused little enthusiasm. A revival of Petipa's *Daughter of Pharaoh* was announced for the benefit of Evgenia Sokolova, but for many the forthcoming debut of Virginia Zucchi in December was the only point of interest. During the opening weeks of the season the theatre was half empty at ballet performances, and when Sokolova injured her leg at a rehearsal, the management took fright and sent Virginia an urgent telegram, begging her to come to St. Petersburg a fortnight earlier, on November 13th. She had no other engagements that prevented her from complying with this request, and to everyone's relief she arrived in the Russian capital, eager to cooperate, though a little jaded after a train journey lasting several days. It was only then that she was told that she was expected to play the title role in *Daughter of Pharaoh* in less than a fortnight's time—a very different undertaking from the familiar part of Lise in *La Fille mal gardée*. Her first reaction was to refuse, but once the subject of the ballet was explained to her, she began to see its possibilities. With her confidence returning, she drove straight from the station to the Imperial School of Ballet, where Petipa was waiting for her.

Benois remembered the stir that her arrival caused. "Many rumours circulated about the rehearsals and preparations for this ballet," he wrote. "According to some, the great Marius had fre-

quent fits of despair about Zucchi, for she did not coincide with
his conception of an ideal dancer. He greatly appreciated a certain
severity and reserve—classicism in the full meaning of the term—
and demanded, above all, absolute subordination to his own ideas.
With Zucchi this was difficult; her temperament generally got the
upper hand in spite of her goodwill, and she always put too much
fire, too much passion into everything she did. The other rumour
was that Petipa was raving about her, even more so her partner,
P. A. Gerdt, so that the rehearsals took place in an atmosphere of
mutual delight. It is probable that both these rumours had some
truth in them, but it seems that only at the beginning things did
not run quite smoothly, as they did later on when the artists had
learned to know each other, and Petipa had realised what a guarantee of success lay in the exceptional temperament of the artiste;
while she, for her part, had understood what was wanted of her.
It was then that the rehearsals began to improve."[3]

There was still one important decision for her to make before her debut on the Imperial stage. She sought out Skalkovsky
and asked him for his considered advice, as a friend. Would it be
better to take along to the theatre cognac or madeira? It was an
unsual problem, and he pondered thoughtfully before giving his reply—"Both."

She no doubt felt in great need of courage for the formidable undertaking that lay before her. Apart from the prestige attach-
ing to the Imperial Theatres, the quality of the *corps de ballet,* and
the high standards by which she would be judged there, she had to
assume a lengthy role in a ballet she did not know with less than a
fortnight's preparation.

Daughter of Pharaoh was one of Petipa's earliest successes.
He had produced it originally in 1862 for Carolina Rosati. It had a
score by the prolific Cesare Pugni, and Saint-Georges' scenario was
distantly inspired by Théophile Gautier's *Le Roman de la momie.*

It told of an opium-inspired dream of an English explorer, Lord Wilson, who has taken shelter from a storm in a pyramid. Aspiccia, the daughter of a pharaoh of old, materialises from a mummy, and Wilson is transported into the past, assuming the form of an ancient Egyptian, Ta-Hor. The scene changes to a wooded valley, where Aspiccia is playing with her attendants while her father is away lion-hunting. A roar is heard, and a lion attacks the princess. Ta-Hor rushes to her defence and kills the beast. He and Aspiccia fall in love, but the pharaoh plans to marry her to the King of Nubia. The lovers flee from the court and seek shelter in a fisherman's hut. The King of Nubia follows them in disguise, and to escape from him Aspiccia throws herself into the Nile.

In an underwater scene the drowned Aspiccia is received by the King of the Nile, and in the form of an undine dances with the spirits of the rivers. She begs to be restored to life so that she can be reunited with Ta-Hor, and the river king relents and releases her. Meanwhile Ta-Hor has been arrested, and is being threatened with death by snake-bite unless he reveals the whereabouts of the princess. At the critical moment Aspiccia returns and denounces the Nubian king for attacking her in the hut. Seeing Ta-Hor being led to his death, she begs for his life. The pharaoh is at first unyielding, but when he sees her about to plunge her arm into the basket containing the snake, he relents. The lovers are united, and a festival brings the dream of the past to a close.

The interest aroused by the announcement of Virginia's debut in this ballet was enormous, reaching the uncommitted public as well as producing a complicated web of partisan intrigue in the small world of the *coulisses.* All the seats were sold within a few hours, and those who were unlucky at the box-office had to pay the touts up to 20 roubles for a three-rouble ticket. On the evening of November 22nd the Bolshoi Theatre was filled to capacity for her debut on the Imperial stage. Not for many years had such a well-dressed audience assembled for the ballet, and its dispersal afterwards resembled, for the brilliance of the uniforms and toilettes, the departure after a ball in the Winter Palace.

It was one of those great theatrical evenings that are remembered both as rare experiences and as turning points. All the shortcomings of the production were overshadowed by the original performance of Virginia Zucchi. From the Imperial Box the deep voice of the Grand Duke Vladimir was heard shouting "Bravo Zucchi!" The old guard of balletomanes, with its excessive regard for tradition—"the ballet ant-heap," as it was called—was thrown into utter confusion, for the Italian ballerina was performing in a style that was completely novel, perpetrating deviations which to their blinkered eyes were inadmissible on a serious stage. But a spark had been kindled, and Pavel Gerdt, who was playing the dual role of Wilson and Ta-Hor, seemed almost unrecognisably inspired. Though many would be reluctant to admit it, ballet in Russia would never be quite the same again.

What no one could deny was that a star of the first magnitude had appeared. Long afterwards Benois could still bring her appearance to his mind in almost every detail. "She could in no case be called beautiful," he wrote, "but she was *mieux que belle et mieux que jolie.* Her eyes had a somewhat Chinese slant, but could widen and sparkle at the proper occasions; her mouth was large, with perfect teeth; her jet black hair was unruly and could not be coaxed into any style of coiffure. At supremely dramatic moments Zucchi made clever use of this artistic untidiness of her hair, for she would push it up with a perfectly natural gesture, and the effect was wonderful. She had an unusually thin natural waist— Zucchi never wore a corset—and a very flexible body with a small chest, round hips and not very slim but perfectly shaped legs. All this created an image which does not correspond to the modern idea of 'beautiful line,' but was extremely attractive nevertheless. Zucchi's back and shoulders were her chief beauty—they were truly perfect. Skalkovsky used to assure us that Zucchi's back contained a whole world of poetry. But her charm had nothing to do with any one of her features. It lay in her wonderful radiant femininity."[4]

The role of Aspiccia was not perhaps the most suitable choice. "Her mime scenes and variations," observed Skalkovsky in *Novoye Vremya*, "were spread thinly in the over-all production, and could not make the impression that would have been achieved had she first appeared in a smaller-scale work such as *La Fille mal gardée*, in which she would have been on stage most of the time."[5] The *Journal de St. Pétersbourg* made a similar comment, while Benois stated that the part of a king's daughter did not suit her character. She was too much nature's child, he explained, and more suited to roles of simple, naive and impulsive heroines. At times her Italian vivacity could appear trivial, but it never failed to charm and he had to admit that her interpretation of the part of Aspiccia was perfect.

Her debut was a considerable triumph, but many critics had reservations, for her style of dancing and her method of miming were very unconventional. On the subject of her dancing the critic of *Novosti* was particularly severe. He reproached her for lacking some of the basic qualities. "In the course of the whole ballet," he wrote, "Mlle. Zucchi performed no *batterie*, not a single *brisé* or *cabriole*, nor a jump; not once did she rise from the floor, and the cleanness of her poses and the beauty of her attitudes in adagio did not make up for this. Delicate *pointes* at the end of bow legs, a few *ronds de jambe* and turns such as are performed by the male dancers Gerdt and Karsavin (but never by *danseuses*, who are trained from childhood in exclusively aesthetic movements) comprise the entire technical equipment of Mlle. Zucchi."[6] The *Teatralny Mirok* reproached her for a lack of good schooling and also noted the absence of elevation and *ballon*. Skalkovsky, however, countered these criticisms by asking how one judges if a ballerina comes from a good school. In Virginia's dancing, he claimed, there was "a com-

plete harmony in every part of the body, an essential assurance of
movement, perfect skill and balance, together with the ability to
appear natural in the least pose so that at every moment she might
serve as a model for an artist or a sculptor. . . . Zucchi is reproached
for the animation and fire of her dancing, on the ground that this
is not classical. But stiffness and good schooling have nothing in
common. Zucchi dances with freedom because she is a *demi-carac-
tere* dancer. . . . It is quite true that she does not belong to the cate-
gory of *ballonné* dancers, but to reproach her for this would be as
unjust as criticising a soprano for not being a contralto. . . . With
Zucchi, the quality I value most is not her technical strength—many
other ballerinas equal her in this—but the soul and wit that she displays in her dancing. Every one of her dances, even the least of
them, satisfied Didelot's requirement that it should be a complete
poem, the content of which must be clear to the audience, and not
a mere collection of acrobatic movements."[7] The *Sanktpeterburgskiye Vedomosti* agreed that her expressiveness made up for her
lack of elevation, and called her "in the full sense of the word, *une
charmeuse.* "[8]

Sergei Khudekov, in the reasoned judgment that he published in his *History of Dancing*, was more severe. Her forte, he
stated, lay in her exceptionally strong *pointes.* Many of her variations included long promenades on the *pointes* that came as a revelation to the Russian ballerinas, who were conditioned not to go
beyond what they were taught in their training. In a short time they
were to assimilate this extension of technique just as successfully as
they were later to discover the secret of multiple *fouettés*. While ap-
preciating the temperament that Virginia displayed in her variations,
Khudekov found much to criticise in her style. "Her turns and arabesques lacked classical charm," he specified. "She sought to shock
by the speed of her movements. She really did turn and spin quickly, hardly rising from the ground and with a complete disregard for
correctness or beauty of line in her unsteady body. . . . Her one

thought was that her variations should always end with her hair
disarranged."[9]

In *Daughter of Pharaoh* she was most successful in the
graceful variation on the *pointes* in the vision scene, and least so in
the oriental *pas de sabre*, which had been created for Marie S.
Petipa. Choreographically, the highlight of the ballet was the *grand
pas d'action* in which Aspiccia and Ta-Hor plan their escape, "a
perfect example of Petipa's art," as Benois called it, in which the
dance was "imperatively united to the development of the plot."
In this Virginia, who had not been wholly convincing as a royal
princess when the King of Nubia was presented to her, "had an
opportunity of displaying a whole gamut of feelings. She tried to
resist Ta-Hor, shuddered at the thought that their flight would
arouse her father's anger, and then, little by little, gave way to the
persuasion of her fiery lover and of her followers. All this has to be
clearly interpreted so that the side-play is obvious to the audience,
while remaining hidden from the two feasting rulers."[10]

Other opportunities to display her sensational dramatic
talent were scattered throughout the ballet: in the prologue she
made an immediate impression when she stepped out from the
mummy and came into the view of the balletomanes for the first
time, "her whole being radiant with happiness."[11] In the first act
she had a sprightly little scene chasing a monkey. The animal was
played by a fourteen-year-old pupil of the ballet school, Nicolai
Legat, who was to remember the experience all his life. A few
moments later this mood of playfulness gave way to terror and
panic when Aspiccia finds herself faced by the lion. Here there was
an unforgettable moment when Virginia crossed the stage pursued
by the beast. "The miming and acting of Zucchi were so convincing
that watching her gave one a sensation of fear," recalled Peter
Lieven many years later. "And this, even although the lion which
pursued her was grotesque in the extreme. The rough cardboard
dummy of a lion, with sagging legs, as if going through the steps of

a foxtrot, slung on crude wires, was dangled over the stage. Yet Zucchi had only to appear, even with this caricature of a lion, to send a shiver down the spine of the spectator." [12]

Another opportunity of displaying her dramatic gifts followed in the scene set in the fisherman's hut, where Aspiccia, pretending to be a simple fisherwoman, describes how she and her lover were overtaken by a storm on the Nile, and later—when the Nubian king appears and forces his unwelcome attentions on her—throws herself into the river. But the most dramatic passage of all was reserved for the last act, where Aspiccia describes the Nubian king's brutality in vivid mime and begs her father to spare her lover. Despairing of moving him, she threatens to take her life by offering her arm to the venomous snake, and then, when the pharaoh at last relents, is overcome with the most ecstatic joy.

Deep as was the impression she created, even her miming did not escape criticism, for it was hardly less unorthodox than her dancing. Some spectators were shocked by the realism of her facial expressions and by the sexuality inherent in the scenes with her lover. Accustomed to a more oblique style of acting, they found her mime scenes conventional and monotonous, her gestures over-sharp and unaesthetic. But the impact remained of an electric personality that compelled immediate attention. Virginia's radiance, wrote Benois, "was expressed most vividly in her face. [Her] capacity for expressing shades of emotion was really remarkable. At the same time her face was extraordinarily suitable for the stage. . . . Some beautiful faces are entirely lost on the stage, for one has to depend on strong opera glasses to discover their admirable qualities. No opera glasses were needed to see Zucchi's face, and to admire every fleeting expression of it." [13]

Her striving for realism was the cause of a brush with Marius Petipa after the first performance. In the scene where Aspiccia is chased by the lion, Virginia added to the effect by tearing off her head-dress, pulling down her hair and disarranging her clothes, allowing her companions to pull her, half fainting, out of the water. Petipa was appalled.

"How could you, a princess, think of appearing before the audience in such an untidy state?" he remonstrated.

"Untidy, why not?"

"Where was your crown?"

"In the water, of course. Where else would it be?"

"But you are a princess. You ought not to be without it!"

"My crown I lost in the water," she retorted with a smile. "And I can tell you this, M. Petipa—had you been pursued by a lion, you would have lost not only your crown, but your trousers, too!" [14]

Virginia was never afraid of revealing her charms. Her tousled hair and the realism of her love scenes gave an erotic touch to her performances, and this was heightened by the very revealing costume she wore in the last act. The critic of the *Teatralny Mirok* was aghast at its transparency and low *décolleté*. Such an exhibition, he declared, had never been seen at the Bolshoi Theatre before. It shook to the very core his notion of ballet as an essentially artificial spectacle with strict aesthetic standards. "Now everything is suddenly turned upside down," he bewailed. [15] She had created a revolution in more ways than one.

The Italian fashion was for much shorter skirts than were worn in Russia at the time of her arrival. She had very decided views on the subject, and when the wardrobe mistress had shown her the costume she was expected to wear, she revolted at the idea of appearing in a skirt of such an outmoded length.

"Cut it shorter at once," she commanded.

"Impossible. This is the regulation length," was the reply.

"Absurd!" Virginia retorted. "I cannot dance in that."

The issue had to be referred to higher authority, but the answer came back that the length of the skirt was regulated by Imperial control.

Virginia said nothing, but on the evening of her debut she took matters into her own hands and cut her skirts well above her knees. "I will have my skirts short," she insisted. "I will not dance in a costume fit for a grandmother."[16]

Not surprisingly, the shorter length was welcomed by most of the balletomanes, and as time went by Virginia felt emboldened to cut her skirts shorter and shorter until finally the Italian fashion quietly imposed itself.

The public demand for seats did not diminish, and more than 11,000 roubles poured into the box office for her first four appearances. At her second performance the Tsar and the Tsarina were present to see her for themselves. On November 29th Sokolova appeared as Aspiccia, and inevitably the two ballerinas were compared and bitter argument broke out. A great clamour went forth from the partisans of the Russian ballerina, who even justified their attitude on the grounds of patriotism! "Only by patriotism," commented Pleshcheyev drily, "can it be shown that cooking sherry is much better than the real thing."[17] The *Sanktpeterburgskiye Vedomosti* called Sokolova's appearance "a complete success for Mlle. Zucchi."[18] The general opinion was, however, that while Sokolova made less of an impression than her Italian rival, she gave a charming performance and was even preferred in some of the dances. But, sadly, she was so discouraged by the unwelcome comparisons that she resolved to retire from the stage and devote herself to teaching. At about the same time it was reported that Nikitina had expressed a similar intention, but happily she was persuaded to change her mind.

Skalkovsky's opinion that Virginia Zucchi should have made her debut on the Imperial stage in *La Fille mal gardée* was now to be vindicated. Petipa's new version of this familiar old ballet, using the Hertel score, was presented on December 27th at a special performance to celebrate the twenty-fifth jubilee of Pavel Gerdt, and in the part of Lise Virginia obtained a triumph of splendid proportions. She and Gerdt, who in the role of Colas was obviously greatly inspired by her performance, gave the ballet new life and vigour.

Notwithstanding the change of music, Petipa had preserved the role
of Lise so as to evoke, in the memory of older spectators, the tradition of Fanny Elssler's great interpretation of some thirty-five years
before. Like Elssler, Virginia brought Lise to life with an insight
and a truth that gave unusual depth to a part that, in the hands of
a lesser artist, could easily appear insubstantial. The impression was
heightened by the power of her communication—"her extraordinary
explicitness in the transmission of feeling."[19] This was most marked
in the third scene, in which Lise slowly succumbs to Colas's impor-
tunity. Benois described her performance in this scene as "strikingly sincere and realistic. . . . Here was a genuinely inexperienced girl
who first felt the danger of temptation and then, moved by her
passion for Colas, gave in to his tender entreaties without losing her
charming shyness. Some people might say that this was a subject
for 'nasty old men' because the very youthfulness of the heroine—
the forty-year-old Zucchi* gave the full illusion of being fifteen—
gave a kind of piquancy to what was going on on the stage and also
to what was hidden from the spectators' eyes—at a certain moment
Lise's mother locks her up in a loft where Colas has concealed himself."[20] Some critics had reservations. D. V. Averkiev thought she
was exquisite, but detected in her portrayal a cunning that was too
calculating and passionate, a quality to be found in a mature woman
rather than a young girl.[21] The critic of *Novosti* took a similar view,
suggesting that Virginia had distorted the role by presenting Lise as
a "cunning, spoilt and passionate girl" instead of a "primitive, ill-
bred (but not spoilt), playful, simple girl" who was full of childish
innocence.[22]

Virginia's dances were designed to show off her technique
and included several feats that were new to St. Petersburg. But these
tours de force were woven with genuine feeling and significance into
a performance that enchanted all who saw it.

*She was, of course, only thirty-six.

The *pas de ruban* in the first act was performed entirely on the *pointes*. It began with Lise circling the stage at the end of a ribbon held by Colas, and then developed into a game of hobby-horse with Colas holding both ends of the ribbon and Lise, as if in the reins, pawing the ground like a skittish little horse. Although it was criticised for a certain lack of taste, it expressed a childish grace and the playfulness of two young people whose hearts have not yet responded to love.

The second scene contained an interpolated *pas de deux* to the music of a well-known Italian romance, "Stella Confidente." It was, in Skalkovsky's phrase, "a *chef d'oeuvre* of choreographic art."[23] In it Virginia performed a brilliant sequence of double *fouettés* on *pointe*, then circled the stage with astonishing cleanness and lightness, and finished with a startling *tour de force,* throwing herself into the arms of her partner, who lifted her at arm's length above his head. None of these difficulties seemed out of place in the portrayal of her role. "Every step," wrote Benois, "seemed to be a declaration of the feelings of an innocent young girl to her beloved."[24] Virginia's performance in this *pas* moved many spectators to tears, and Benois remembered how the sculptor Aubert, an old friend of his family, had to retire to the privacy of the avant-loge and there wept unashamedly.

The ballet ended in a burst of gaiety, with Virginia and Gerdt dancing a *polka de caractère* and *bourrée*. When the performance was over, wreaths and gifts were presented and Petipa made a speech, but the gesture that brought the house down was when Virginia threw her arms impulsively around Gerdt and kissed him when he declared, in his speech of thanks, that the art of ballet knew no national boundaries.

Here, symbolised by this embrace, was the coming together of two schools of ballet, from which the Russian style of the twentieth century was to develop. As Virginia's partner, Gerdt felt her influence more immediately than anyone else, and as one of the principal teachers in the Imperial School he was to pass it on to others. He acknowledged his indebtedness to her inspiration to the end of his days. "Working with Zucchi," he would say, "had opened my eyes to many things." [25]

For Virginia's benefit on February 26th Marius Petipa arranged—in the space of less than a fortnight—a new ballet called *The King's Command* to a score by Albert Vizentini. The plot was borrowed from Delibes' opera *Le Roi l'a dit,* but with the setting transposed from the France of Louis XIV to the Spain of Philip II to enable Spanish dances to be introduced in addition to historical dances such as gavottes, chaconnes and pavanes. The action revolves around the dilemma of the Count de la Sierra, when he receives a long-coveted command from the King to present himself at court with his son and is too timid to reveal that he only has four daughters. To resolve the problem he takes with him his maid Pepita's sweetheart, Marguino. They are followed by Pepita, who manages to gain admittance to a royal ball where she flirts with her sweetheart. The Count's deception is revealed at last, and all ends happily with the King forgiving the Count on condition that his daughters are given to the young men of their choice.

The character of Pepita, which was envisaged as a kind of female Figaro, full of vivacity, high spirits and witty ingenuity, ought to have suited Virginia's temperament and interpretative talent perfectly. But, through no fault of hers, it was not fully developed: the opportunities for building up the character were too few and too scattered. There was an amusing moment in the first act when she brings her sweetheart out from under a table where he has been hidden, there was an opportunity to express despair when he leaves to go to court with his master, and an interesting transition from grief to joy when he feigns death and suddenly springs to life before her, but these incidents were somewhat submerged by all the divertissements and the rather arid period dances.

It was not one of Petipa's more inventive ballets, but his choreography interestingly revealed a prompt and positive reaction to the developed *pointe* work of the Italian school, for several of the Russian dancers were allowed for the first time to attempt feats of this order. There were, of course, technical difficulties woven into Virginia's own dances—in particular, a multiple pirouette taken slowly on the *pointe* in the *pas de paon*—but Petipa also sought to bring out her interpretative qualities. This was most notable in the entrancing *Tirana,* a Spanish dance with Moorish overtones that she performed "with great chic," and in the *Charmeuse*, full of passion and vivacity, that concluded with an almost acrobatic pose on her partner's shoulders.

The ballet itself was a failure, but the evening was a triumph for Virginia. Exactly by how much it enriched her the records do not reveal. In accordance with her contract she received from the theatre 2,324 roubles and 40 kopecks, but this took no account of the profit which she herself made by selling tickets. It was the custom for a dancer taking a benefit to take nearly all the seats herself at the prices agreed with the theatre and to retail these at as great a profit as she could exact. It was here that Virginia depended on the balletomanes, and Nicolai Bezobrazov in particular. Bezobrazov, who in his old age was to advise Diaghilev, was then a comparatively young man. But with his intimate knowledge of St. Petersburg society, he knew better than anyone how to distribute the seats to best advantage; and he was notoriously adept at shaming people into paying enormous premiums and in addition making a donation for a gift to be presented publicly on the stage. Virginia's profit from this "black market" can only be guessed at: it was reported that she had rejected an offer from some touts to take all the seats at double the agreed price, and that people were paying her 50, 100, and even 300 roubles for boxes.

The ovations that punctuated the performance that evening were convincing testimony of St. Petersburg's adulation. At the end

Virginia Zucchi in her dressing room.
(Museo alla Scala, Milan)

Julián Gayarre, the Spanish tenor. Photo: Chalot.
(Musée de l'Opéra, Paris)

The Kin Grust pleasure gardens in St. Petersburg, 1885. Top: a general view from the river; upper centre: Virginia Zucchi; centre left: the theatre in which Zucchi made her first appearance in Russia; below: the Chinese garden. Engraved from drawings by A. Ryabushkin. *(Victoria and Albert Museum, London)*

Virginia Zucchi in her celebrated variation on the *pointes*, danced by her at Kin Grust, St. Petersburg, in 1885. *(Bakhrushin Theatre Museum, Moscow)*

Zucchi as Padmana in the dagger scene in Monplaisir's *Brahma* (Kin Grust, St. Petersburg, 1885). *(Bakhrushin Theatre Museum, Moscow)*

Scenes from Petipa's *Daughter of Pharoah* at the Bolshoi Theatre, St. Petersburg, 1885. Top: the mummy comes to life. Lower left: Tao-Hor rescues Aspiccia from the lion. Centre right: Aspiccia about to throw herself into the Nile. Lower right: Aspiccia pleads with the Pharoah to spare Tao-Hor. Engraved from drawings by P. A. Grigoriev. *(Victoria and Albert Museum, London)*

Two photographs of Virginia Zucchi as Lise in *La Fille mal gardee* (Bolshoi Theatre, St. Petersburg, 1885). Photos: Bergamasco. *(Bakhrushin Theatre Museum, Moscow)*

Virginia Zucchi in *The King's Command*
(Bolshoi Theatre, St. Petersburg, 1885).
Photo: Bergamasco. *(Soviet Archives)*

Scenes from the 1887 revival of Petipa's *The King's Command* at the Maryinsky Theatre, St. Petersburg.
In the oval frame, upper left: **Pavel Gerdt** and **Virginia Zucchi.** Engraved from drawings by K. Brozh.
(Victoria and Albert Museum, London)

of the second act the enthusiasm rose to an extraordinary pitch.
Again and again she was called before the curtain, and young Alexandre Benois, who was in the theatre wearing his first dress-coat in
honour of his goddess, was interested to observe her novel manner
of thanking the public. Not for her the conventional *révérence*, as
taught at the Imperial School. When she acknowledged the applause,
"she expressed by her gestures, her eyes, and her whole figure how
deeply moved she was by such appreciation, how she reciprocated
the feelings, how she *loved* her audience." [26] As she stood bowing,
bouquets, wreaths and baskets of flowers bearing ribbons with such
inscriptions as "Bravo Diva" were handed to her across the orchestra pit until the front of the stage resembled a garden. The tributes
were not all just floral. One of the baskets was reported to contain
a fur coat. The conductor of the orchestra also handed up to her
more precious gifts—a silver garland, a diamond and ruby brooch,
a diamond diadem—but the climax came when she opened a case
to reveal a necklace of enormous diamonds. The audience gasped
as the stones sparkled in the light. It was a gift from her most
extravagant admirer, Prince B. Vassilchikov. Many spectators recognised these jewels as the famous Kachinsky diamonds and were
deeply shocked that such a precious family treasure should be
presented to a theatrical artist, and a foreigner at that. Naturally
hidden motives were suspected, and one wit, playing on the
double meaning of the word *rivière*, commented that it was
"une rivière qui cherche son lit."
    The climax of this remarkable evening took place in the
fashionable restaurant of the Pivato Frères in Morskaya Street, near
Maryinskaya Square. Here "the oldest balletomane," Arcady Pokhvisnev, welcomed her at the supper table. Raising his glass to pro-
pose her health, he read, in a tone that befitted the solemnity of the
occasion, some verses that described how in days gone by he had
harnessed himself to Fanny Elssler's carriage and helped draw her
through the streets of St. Petersburg in triumph. "And here is a

new genius," he proclaimed, kneeling before Virginia as he asked the company to stand and drink her health. Many speeches and toasts followed, and it was four o'clock in the morning before the party broke up and the exhilarated balletomanes and their goddess emerged into the fresh air and were driven back to their homes.

One may be sure that Virginia did not lose her sense of proportion in the face of all this worship. The divine one was, in fact, refreshingly human. "Her histrionics on stage," recalled Pleshcheyev, "were replaced in real life by a cheerful, boisterous humour. Off stage one seldom saw her pensive, sentimental or serious."[27]

Not surprisingly, she had quickly become a popular figure in St. Petersburg society, taking part in the city's activities to the extent that her professional commitments allowed. She agreed, for example, to play the daggers scene from *Brahma* at a charity show, miming it with her customary energy on a tiny stage, after arriving post-haste from the Bolshoi Theatre, where she had been dancing in *The King's Command.* Few people had the good fortune to meet her in more than a casual way. Many saw her off stage only at some society ball, where she might be asked to sell lottery tickets in the hope that some of the more ardent balletomanes would empty their wallets for her. It was at such a ball that a reporter described her for the readers of the *Teatralny Mirok.* She was, he wrote, "most modestly dressed, pretty and coquettish. Her accent in speaking French is a joy to listen to. The way she pronounces 's' like 'z' delights her admirers, and indeed everyone. Zucchi's coiffure was very elegant, although her detractors had spread the tale that her hair was always untidy, as it is on stage. To everyone his own taste. In our opinion the fashionable coiffures of the hair-dresser in Morskaya Street have no connection with art. Zucchi's hair style is original, but never oversteps the bounds of elegance."[28]

She treated the balletomanes with affectionate familiarity, and they adored her for it. She found their long Russian names almost impossible to cope with, and she shortened those of her two

staunch champions, Skalkovsky and Bezobrazov, to Skalko and
Bezo. Both these men held posts in the Department of Mines, which
seemed almost to have become a Virginia Zucchi admiration society.
At meetings of the Mining Council Skalkovsky often found himself
sitting next to the venerable mineralogist, Academician Koksharov,
who whiled away the time writing impromptu verses. A typical example revealed the direction in which the Council's thoughts were
inclined to turn:

> To banish the boredom
> Of the Council's debates,
> This is what I propose:
> Let's hasten to the ballet—
> The Divine Zucchi is there!

To the effusive outpourings of the balletomanes Virginia
countered with a wit that both delighted them and yet showed that
her head was not to be turned. When Skalkovsky begged her to send
him one of her ballet slippers, she joined in the spirit of the game by
accompanying the offering with the following note, which one
might imagine to have been concocted with the help of Bezo: "The
Secretary *in partibus infidelium* of Mlle. Virginia Zucchi, assuring
Constantin Apollonovich of her complete regard, has the honour on
the instructions of the Prima Ballerina to forward, through him, for
adding to the choreographic records which are kept by the Member
of the Mining Council, a ballet slipper of Virginia Zucchi with an
inscription which, translated into the Russian language, reads thus:
'Remember the points which were in this slipper and that shot the
arrow into your heart.'"[29]

Her engagement was now almost at its end. At her last performance a few days later she was given a wreath with the inscription, "Until the next time, and the sooner the better." Apart from
the artistic consequences of her engagement, the material results

shown by the box-office returns had been little short of miraculous. In her first season on the Imperial stage she had appeared twenty-four times, and these performances had grossed 64,500 roubles, the total takings for the season being about 100,000 roubles—nearly double the corresponding figure for the preceding season. The Imperial Theatres had every reason to be satisfied, and before returning to Milan, she signed a contract to appear for four months of the following season for 12,000 roubles and a benefit, and had already begun preliminary rehearsals of *Esmeralda.*

She was given a splendid farewell at the Warsaw Railway Station and left with flowers filling her compartment and the prayers of her admirers for a speedy return still sounding in her ears.

"Esmeralda"
at the Maryinsky

During the summer of 1886, while Virginia was resting in the Italian sunshine, two of her compatriots followed in her footsteps to relieve the boredom of the balletomanes in the pleasure gardens of St. Petersburg. At Arcadia Antonietta Dell'Era arrived with a small supporting company to present truncated versions of *Coppélia, Giselle* and *Satanella*, while Adelina Sozo came to dazzle the public at the Zoological Gardens. Neither possessed Virginia's interpretative qualities, but their technical virtuosity created a sensation, even though the purists grumbled that it bordered on the acrobatic. Never before had the worn-out cliché "points of steel" been used more appropriately than when applied to the seemingly incredible feats on *pointe* that these two ballerinas performed with such ease and aplomb.

Meanwhile the balletomanes were preparing themselves for Virginia's return to their midst. Her second contract with the Imperial Theatres, which she had signed in January, bound her to give twenty-four performances spread over four months, starting on October 27th. It had been announced that *Esmeralda* and *Excelsior* were to be produced for her and that she was to play the mime role of the heroine in *Fenella*, as the Russians called Auber's opera *La Muette de Portici*. She was also to appear in different surroundings— on the stage of the Maryinsky Theatre, which was now to become the home of the Imperial ballet.

Today the Maryinsky Theatre symbolises in imaginative retrospect the Imperial ballet in its most glorious phase, but in 1886 it was the Bolshoi, where Virginia had made her Russian debut the year before, that stirred the nostalgia of the balletomanes. For the

93

older generation the Bolshoi, with its colonnaded entrance dominat-
ing the centre of Theatre Square, was the true temple of the dance,
dedicated to a succession of goddesses from Taglioni, Elssler and
Andreanova in the distant 1840s to the divine Virginia. The lavish
gilding and the crimson brocade hangings of its six-tiered auditorium had for long provided a setting of solemn splendour for multi-
coloured uniforms and toilettes as the fashionable audiences gathered for the ballet or the Italian opera. And the smell of gas that assailed the nostrils inside the vast, over-heated building only seemed
to add to its atmosphere of mystery like a rare and exotic incense.
But now, in 1886, the old theatre stood forlorn and abandoned,
condemned to demolition as no longer safe, and the dancers were
moving across the Square to the more modern surroundings of the
Maryinsky, where electricity shed a brighter, less odorous and less
intimate light.

The Maryinsky stood on the site of a small theatre that had
been burned down in 1859. At that time the Imperial Theatres
needed another stage to present Russian opera, and the court architect, Albert Cavos, designed the new theatre, which was given the
name of the Maryinsky, after the Empress of Alexander II, when it
was opened in 1860. In 1885, when the decision was made to move
the ballet from the Bolshoi, a number of improvements were carried
out to make it worthy of the Imperial court that supported it: an
electricity power plant was installed, and the building was enlarged
to include a green room, a second scene-painting workshop, a photo-
graphic studio, a scenery store, a carpenter's shop and more offices.
The design and colour scheme of the auditorium provided a strong
contrast to the sombre Bolshoi. It was, wrote one who remembered
it, "very magnificent in a rococo style, done in cream and blue
natier, which harmonised with the gilt bas-reliefs. There was a great
deal of velvet and soft hangings, and a huge chandelier of cut crystal
lit up the whole auditorium."[1] The consideration that had been giv-
en to the audience's comfort could be gauged from the seating capa-

city, which, in spite of its size, was no more than 1,625. The reopening had taken place in February 1886, with a production of an extravaganza called *Les Pilules du Diable*, for which Petipa had arranged the incidental ballets, but it was not until the opening of the 1886–87 season in September that the ballet was to take up permanent residence there.

For a time it had been feared that Virginia might not return. A disturbing rumour arose that she was about to marry a millionaire landowner—perhaps the friend with whom it was reported she had stayed, at his estate in the province of Vilna, on her way back to Italy in the summer—and retire from the stage. To everyone's relief this was denied, and she arrived in St. Petersburg punctually in accordance with her contract. Her admirers were hungry for news of her, and even the most trivial detail was deemed worthy of record by the *Teatralny Mirok* when it reported a reception she gave for her admirers.

"The balletomanes were of course present," it began. "One over-familiar gentleman, clasping his hands, grew specially excited and babbled about her toes. As an alternative to descriptions such as "steely," "candy-sweet," and "like gutta-percha," someone suggested "like Lisle thread." It was objected that this did not signify because Lisle thread had an unpleasant smell. This was confirmed by one of the balletomanes. 'My socks,' he exclaimed with pathetic ecstasy, 'smell very strong. . . . particularly in the evening when I go out, but in the morning I find they do not smell any more.' Everyone felt reassured. Virginia has grown much better looking and appears younger. Her face was shown to advantage by a grey plush talma and a black hat with a white veil. She had brought with her an old lady whom the balletomanes at first took to be the divine one's maid. But it appeared that the old lady was a ballerina. They say she will dance on the stage here. Why should she not have a try? The old lady is all of fifty or sixty. That means she is experienced, if not as a dancer, then at least as a woman."[2]

The ballet season opened with *Daughter of Pharaoh*, with Sokolova as Aspiccia. The audience was lethargic, and the houses were half empty during the six weeks before Virginia's appearance on October 27th. By contrast there was not an empty seat to be seen that evening, and the excitement could be sensed as the curtain rose on *La Fille mal gardée*. But the audience had not come to indulge in uncritical enthusiasm. Since her last appearance a new star had risen, and many balletomanes were now curious to judge her in the afterglow of Dell'Era's brilliance. Virginia clearly sensed this, for she was visibly nervous. It was noticed, too, despite what the *Teatralny Mirok* had reported, that her physical charms seemed to have diminished: she had become pinched and thin, both in face and in figure, and her shoulders had acquired a sharpness in quite a tell-tale way."[3] The applause at her first entrance was a little subdued, but her success grew as the evening wore on. If she could not match Dell'Era's elevation and technical finish, or her marvellous feats on the *pointes* and her triple turns, she quickly reestablished her supremacy as a dancer-actress. According to the *Journal de St. Pétersbourg,* "every step and every movement has a meaning that can be fully comprehended, and in the great love scene in the third act she makes an impact as only a great dramatic artist disposing of all the resources of speech and declamation could do. As a dancer too Mlle. Zucchi performed real marvels, particularly in the *pas de deux* of the second act. It is difficult to say which was the more astonishing—the delicate variations on *pointe*,. . . the sequence of eighteen turns performed in one breath on the *pointe* of one foot,* or the leap into Gerdt's arms. The rhythm of the polka often returns in this ballet: we like the humourous polka in the last scene,

---

*Can this be a reference to anything other than a long sequence of *fouettés*? If so, it antedates the earliest reference to Legnani's famous feat of thirty-two (in the London *Sketch* of April 26th, 1893) by seven years. Carlotta Zambelli remembered seeing Maria Giuri performing multiple *fouettés* some time before Legnani went to Russia.

but we prefer the quasi-martial polka of the first act that the charming ballerina performs with tense precision."[4]

A few days later she reappeared in *Daughter of Pharaoh*. The previous year she had had little success with the *pas de sabre*, which Petipa had originally created for his wife, Marie S. Petipa. This she now replaced with a new *variation orientale* that she arranged herself to new music by Riccardo Drigo. She judged the reaction of the audience to a nicety, for there was just the right mixture of graceful plastic movement and strong *pointe* work, and the *pas* was encored. In the context of the role of Aspiccia, which demanded dramatic as well as dancing ability, the argument about the respective merits of herself and Dell'Era continued. No one disputed the purely technical superiority of Dell'Era, but not everyone accepted that Virginia's realistic miming was suited to ballet. Her own supporters, however, maintained that "she brought out the inner substance of ballet that till now had played only a very small part," and observed that "a section of the audience used to leave the auditorium during the mime scenes of a ballet, but now they are so gripped that they remain in their seats."[5]

The hasty revival of the old ballet *Paquita* on November 14th attracted little notice. Although it had been intermittently performed for some forty years, it had never been really successful, but now, thanks to Virginia's presence, it attracted full houses for the first time. Virginia had not had time to absorb the part fully; although she had mastered the mime passages, the only dance she was able to learn thoroughly was the *cachucha*, which she performed in the second act with Kshesinski and Gerdt. In her interpretation this acquired a dramatic significance it had lacked before. For her other variations, she inserted dances that had been seen before: in the first act, a variation to a Strauss waltz that she had performed in *Les Pommes d'or* at Kin Grust and, in the ballroom scene in Act III, the *pas de voile* from *Brahma*. This latter dance now included a striking effect that Adelina Sozo had introduced at the Zoological Gardens in the summer—a *pas de bourrée* performed on a moving

strip of material. And this was followed by a "sequence of very difficult pirouettes, *échappés* and *fouettés* and all kinds of balletic
devilry. . . that Mlle. Zucchi performed with such ease and fascination that some old gentlemen had to be taken out of the theatre
half dead with excitement, and young men learnt more in an evening than from twenty-five years of study."[6] From all this Skalkovsky drew the moral that the prerequisite for box-office success was
not an increased administrative staff, nor a splendid production,
nor even a new theatre, but a talented performer.

All this was only the prelude for the production that everyone was waiting for. *Esmeralda*, Jules Perrot's great ballet based on
Victor Hugo's novel, *Notre Dame de Paris,* had not been performed
in St. Petersburg for fourteen years, but there were experienced balletomanes who remembered well some of the greatest interpretations—that of Fanny Elssler above all, which some of the oldest had
seen; the more restrained performance of Carlotta Grisi, who had
created the part in London; and the dramatic rendering of Praskovia
Lebedeva—golden memories all, against which Virginia's interpretation would be judged. In contrast to the penny-pinching treatment
of *Paquita*, new sets and costumes had been prepared for this revival of *Esmeralda*, and both the choreography and the music had
been thoroughly revised. The young Italian conductor, Riccardo
Drigo, had been given the opportunity of proving his ability as a
composer not only by revising Cesare Pugni's score but by writing
new music for a dramatic *pas de six* that was to replace Perrot's *pas
d'action* in the third act and provide Virginia with a "show piece"
of expressive dancing. It was an inspiring challenge, which he met
so successfully that his music aroused great enthusiasm when first
heard in rehearsal.

This new production of *Esmeralda* was first given at Virginia's benefit performance on December 29th, 1886. "The theatre," it was reported, "was absolutely full. All St. Petersburg was
present in ostentatious strength. In the boxes of the *bel étage* and

the first tier* splendid toilettes, as at a *bal paré,* were in evidence, and the brilliant sparkle of diamonds competed with the electric lights of the auditorium. Evening dress and white stiff shirts prevailed in the parterre. Present were almost all the members of the diplomatic corps, the aristocracy of birth and high finance, all the lovers of the ballet and, of course, all the balletomanes in their full complement, severe connoisseurs and judges *par excellence.*"[7]

If just one interpretation had to be singled out as representing the quintessence of Virginia Zucchi's art, there can be little doubt that the choice would fall on her Esmeralda. It was on this role that critics allowed their pens to linger most, describing many of the nuances of characterisation that thrilled the audience by their insight and truth. By piecing together the contemporary accounts of this performance a vivid understanding of her art can be glimpsed, even though it must now lack the immediacy of visual experience.

The action of the ballet was set in the Paris of the fifteenth century. In the first act the gypsy heroine Esmeralda makes a carefree appearance in a colourful street scene, to find the penniless poet Pierre Gringoire at the mercy of a crowd of beggars whose self-styled king has decreed he must die because he possesses nothing worth stealing. By the unwritten law of beggars he can be spared if he finds a woman willing to marry him. Moved by his plight, Esmeralda agrees to marry him, and the scene develops into a round of brilliant dancing. A lascivious priest, Claude Frollo, has conceived a passion for her, and he and the hunchbacked bell-ringer of Notre Dame,Quasimodo, seize her when she crosses the square alone in the fading light. They are thwarted by the approach of the patrol, whose captain, Phoebus, is so taken by the charms of the girl whom he has rescued that he gives her his scarf and begs a kiss. Her heart filled

*The first tier was the lowest tier of all, and the *bel étage* the one immediately above, on a level with the Imperial box—what we should call the dress circle.

with thoughts of the handsome captain, Esmeralda makes her way to her lodging. There she has to deal with her other admirers: Gringoire, whom she informs that she has married only out of pity, and Frollo, from whose unwelcome embraces she manages to break free.

The third act takes place in the garden of a wealthy mansion, where the forthcoming marriage of Phoebus and his high-born bride is being celebrated. Esmeralda appears as one of a band of gypsies engaged to entertain the guests. The sight of Phoebus engaged to another is a shattering blow, but she forces herself to dance, supported by the faithful Gringoire. Phoebus is so moved by her plight that he secretly meets her in a cabaret and declares his love. But unknown to them, Frollo is concealed in the room. He bursts upon them; there is a struggle and a flash of steel. Frollo leaps through the window, and Esmeralda, left alone with the body of her lover, is accused of his murder. She is taken to prison, tortured and led to the scaffold. There Frollo cynically offers to save her if she will give herself to him. She scornfully rejects him. Then, when all seems lost, Phoebus, whom everyone believes to be killed, appears. Esmeralda is saved. In a burst of jealousy Frollo attempts to kill Phoebus, but Quasimodo snatches his dagger and plunges it into the villain's heart.

Supporting Virginia on the evening of her benefit, when St. Petersburg first applauded her Esmeralda, were some of the leading members of the Russian company: Gerdt as the poet Gringoire, Felix Kshesinski as Claude Frollo, Josef Kshesinski (son of Felix and elder brother of the future ballerina Matilda) as Phoebus, and Aladar Bekefy as Quasimodo.

For Virginia's admirer Skalkovsky, her success that evening was a triumph not merely for herself but also for the art of mime itself. "The shade of Noverre," he wrote "must have surely rejoiced in the Elysian fields."[8] His fellow critic Pleshcheyev declared that Fanny Elssler could hardly have surpassed her. Yet when Virginia made her first entrance as the carefree Esmeralda, many felt that her years must tell against her. "The Esmeralda of the early acts must be lighter, younger and more naive than the Italian ballerina was capable of conveying," wrote *Novosti.*[9] Another critic, however, recognised the very character of Victor Hugo's creation—"a girl full of light-hearted merriment who has never been in love and is very good-hearted, and who out of simple kindness has saved the unfortunate Pierre Gringoire from the noose by pretending to be his wife. Observe Zucchi at the first meeting with Phoebus, when her face literally glows with the light of first love—love that has come like a bolt from the blue, love at first sight, the same sort of love, in short, that Shakespeare first revealed to us in *Romeo and Juliet.* Look closely at her face when Phoebus begs her for a kiss. At first she refuses him and keeps him at a distance, her modesty filling her with a feeling of indignation. Then, under the influence of Phoebus's imploring and adoring gaze, her resistance weakens and you perceive, at this moment, an expression, totally aesthetic, of feminine coquetry. Weakening more and more, wishing perhaps to experience the sweetness of her first kiss yet at the same time afraid and doubting her self-control, she runs from the stage."[10]

It was from the third act that her genius really began to shine. The turning point was the scene where Esmeralda, with a troupe of gypsies, comes to dance at a betrothal party. At her first entrance "she is lively and merry and unsuspecting of the grief that lies in store for her at the discovery that the bridegroom is her beloved Phoebus. When the truth dawns, the shock, the sorrow, the depression and the bitterness are communicated through Zucchi's eyes; her features and her whole body are indescribable. She still must dance. She would run away if the fear of scandal did not restrain her, but she controls herself and begins to dance. But only her body is dancing; her spirit has left it and is to be seen only in her feverish gaze which she fixes on her betrayer. The tambourine trembles in her hands. . . At moments her strength seems about to give way, and only Gringoire's encouragement keeps her going. But there is a limit to her endurance. The last drop of energy leaves her, her eyes become glazed and she faints, like a wilted flower, into the arms of Gringoire, who is hardly able to hold her."[11]

All this was expressed in the inspired new *pas de six* that Petipa had arranged to Drigo's music. Impregnated with all the dramatic significance of the heart-breaking situation in which Esmeralda found herself, it was a masterpiece of choreography such as Petipa alone could produce. In the adagio, in which she was partnered by Gerdt—a passage bristling with difficult *tours de force* and performed to a haunting violin solo by Leopold Auer—Virginia had to express the jealousy and hopeless despair of the lovelorn gypsy girl. "This," declared Skalkovsky, "was the ideal of intelligent dancing. If a ballerina can be said to have wit in her legs, then Mlle. Zucchi has it in her whole body, so expressive was every movement."[12] There were some hauntingly beautiful moments when Esmeralda is on the verge of fainting from emotion and Gringoire catches her and, by shaking his tambourine, encourages her to continue dancing. This was followed by a dance by four gypsy girls, and then came Esmeralda's variation, another display of dramatic dancing in which, after a nervous outburst of disdain expressed in technically difficult choreography, Esmeralda moves backwards on her *pointes* in a sort of *pas de bourrée* from the back of the stage to the footlights before dropping into the final pose on one knee. Hopeless sorrow could not have been more movingly expressed.

In the fourth act, in the tavern where Esmeralda and Phoebus meet and declare their love for one another—"a delightful scene"—Virginia had "a wonderfully aesthetic and elegant movement when, on the point of yielding to Phoebus, she pushes him away in a burst of girlish modesty."[13]

As the drama mounted, her acting grew in intensity. In the final scene, when Esmeralda is brought out of prison, barely able to stand after being tortured, the audience's attention was absolute. "You see a woman who has physically changed, who is half dead;

you read in her expression such pathos, such heart-rending sorrow.
She is shattered. Only thus can one describe her grief, her feeling of
outrage against injustice, and withal her resignation, her submissive-
ness to her fate. She is tortured morally as well as physically, but
she is still a young woman and still has such a love of life as to be
filled with horror at the sight of the executioner. She is tempted to
throw herself on the mercy of her bitter enemy, Claude Frollo, and
implore his help, but her spirit conquers her flesh and she begins
to pray and weep. Calling Gringoire to her, she confides to him her
last pathetic wish—to be buried with Phoebus's scarf. When Claude
Frollo approaches her and offers to save her if she will give him her
love, a youthful desire to live blazes up in her again, but only for an
instant. She repulses Claude with a feeling of inexpressible horror
and loathing. Then, when Phoebus, whom everyone has believed to
be dead, appears and revives Esmeralda from her swoon, Zucchi's
face lights up with a look of celestial joy. You then understand that
she is too exhausted, that time has passed by for her, that she can
no longer love as before; and in her look you recognise a feeling of
triumph at the stain of disgrace having been removed rather than an
expression of love, and happiness, but more for Phoebus than for herself. As the curtain falls you want to exclaim: 'Oh, why is she not
a dramatic actress! Give her the gift of words, let her speak! For
she eclipses all tragic actresses, past and present."[14]
     Among the thousands who saw her as Esmeralda at the
Maryinsky were some for whom the experience was to play an important part in shaping their own careers. One of these was Maria
Velizary, who was then beginning to make her name as an actress
in the club theatres of the capital. A connoisseur had told her that,
while Virginia was an excellent mime and a dancer renowned for
her pirouettes and "steel toes," she had one unacceptable fault—she
danced with a bent knee. But when she saw Virginia's Esmeralda,
she found it impossible to quibble over such a petty detail. She was
overwhelmed, and in her memoirs, written many years later, she

recalled the scene where Esmeralda realises that Phoebus is betrothed to another, and the intensity with which Virginia conveyed
the unhappy heroine's torment of jealousy and despair. "During
the dance," she wrote, "Zucchi bends before him, holding her
tambourine close to the ground, and when she raises her face you
see great tears rolling down those beautiful features that are racked
with torment. . . . Never in the straight drama have I ever seen an
actress able to weep so naturally. . . . I have seen Sarah Bernhardt as
Marguerite. When she wrote her letter to Armand, she was lit by a
spotlight. The audience had to see the real tears falling from the
eyes of the great actress. But because these tears seemed too theatrical, they did not move me. But when I saw Zucchi, I saw into
the very depths of the soul of that abandoned, battered character,
and I think everyone else in the audience believed in her too. With
Sarah Bernhardt this was not so. In Zucchi there was genuine emotion, but with Sarah Bernhardt it was just excellent technique." [15]

Another girl on whom Virginia made a deep impression was
Felix Kshesinski's daughter Matilda, who was then a promising pupil
at the Theatre School. Although she was already playing small parts,
she was at this time assailed by doubts whether she had made the
right decision to become a dancer. The experience of Virginia's
Esmeralda came as a revelation at this critical point in her career.
"Zucchi's movements, the line of her arms and back, were astonish-
ingly expressive, and I wanted to seize them, to make a mental photograph of them, greedily following her acting with my still childish eyes. . . . When, in my later career, I danced *Esmeralda,* I was
inspired by memories of her interpretation which, in this ballet, had
reached the most sublime dramatic expression. For me Zucchi was
the genius of dancing, a genius which had inspired and directed me
in the true way at a time when I was still on the verge of adolescence
and about to begin my career." [16]

The child, who was shortly to become the first Russian to be
officially accredited as *prima ballerina assoluta*, was eternally grate-
ful and for many years kept, preserved in spirit, a flower that the

great Italian ballerina once gave her—a precious relic that, to her sorrow, had to be left behind when she fled from Russia during the Revolution.

The realism of Virginia's acting still did not satisfy everyone's tastes. The music critic Hermann Laroche felt that it derogated from the musical foundation of a ballet performance, and Tchaikowsky preferred a ballerina who relied on her dancing to make an effect. But it took a hardened, unsympathetic soul to resist the impact of her full-blooded acting, and one of the very few criticisms of Virginia Zucchi in this branch of her act came from Baron Drizen, written many years afterwards. "I recall a great conventionality—to the detriment of the illusion," he wrote. "In *Esmeralda* there was a scene where the unfortunate girl is being taken to her execution. Probably because of the artist's miming, her admirers punctuated this scene with deafening applause, and Zucchi, without changing her position—she was reclining on a stretcher—forgot the emotion of the part and thanked her audience with charming smiles." [17]

How much she gained from the benefit performance in which she introduced her Esmeralda to St. Petersburg will remain a mystery: it is known that she received from the box office 2,257.30 roubles, but this took no account of the profit she had made on the resale of seats. In addition there were the gifts of flowers and precious jewellery presented to her both during and after the performance. Among the baskets of flowers was one from the Russian ballerina, Evgenia Sokolova, who had taken her retirement benefit a few weeks before. After the performance Virginia presented every member of the company with a box of sweets with an inscribed photograph of herself, and her triumph was celebrated with champagne.

An additional cause for gratification was the presence of the Tsar Alexander III and the Tsarina in the Imperial box. His Majesty had signified his pleasure by going on to the stage afterwards to congratulate Virginia. In his bluff way he had then slapped Drigo heartily on the back, telling him that his music was magnificent and that the orchestra had made great progress under his direction. He was so impressed that his beneficence did not stop there. Shortly afterwards the Director of the Imperial Theatres received an important communication from the Palace. "By Imperial Command," it began, "I have the honour to forward to Your Excellency a bracelet with rubies and diamonds, and a note that this gift is most graciously presented to the ballerina of the Imperial Theatres, Virginia Zucchi, at her benefit, as a keepsake of the visit of Their Imperial Majesties. I beg you to acknowledge its receipt." Vsevolozhsky handed the bracelet to Virginia in his office, and in the margin of the letter from the Imperial Household she neatly wrote: "*Ho ricevuta il magnifico Braccioletto.*"[18]

After *Esmeralda* came *Fenella*, another challenge. Fenella, the dumb heroine of Auber's opera, was one of the touchstones of the art of mime, and once again it was the memory of Fanny Elssler with which Virginia had to contend. In the opera the heroine is caught up in a revolutionary movement, led by her brother Masaniello, in seventeenth-century Naples. The vicissitudes of the unfortunate girl, who is torn between her love for the Viceroy's son and her natural sympathy with the popular cause, provided many dramatic moments.

At the close of the first act, before the church where the marriage of the Viceroy's son Alphonso and the Princess Elvira is being celebrated, Fenella recognises the bridegroom as her seducer and realises she has been betrayed. At the point where Elvira asks Fenella whether she is acquainted with her husband, Virginia replied with a vigorous nod of her head that, in the words of one critic, would be "remembered like one of those sublime words that are uttered from time to time by the great tragedians."[19] A whole range of emotions was expressed in this scene with "such boldness and artistry as would touch the hardest of hearts—outraged pride

and jealousy at the sight of Alphonso married to another, a deep
and infinite grief turning quickly to despair, a struggle between
hatred and the desire to be revenged for her disgrace on the one
hand, and magnanimity and the desire to forgive on the other."[20]

In the following act Fenella's confession of her seduction to
her brother gave Virginia another powerful scene; in the third act
she revealed a gift for choreography with a brilliant arrangement of
the tarantella, in which she and Bekefy led the *corps de ballet*; and
in the fourth act there was another touching scene, when Alphonso
and Elvira throw themselves on Fenella's mercy and she persuades
her brother to assure their safety.

No one could fail to be touched by the realism of Virginia's
miming. "Not even the most minute detail was overlooked," wrote
the critic of *Syn Otechestva.* "Probably everyone has noticed that
particular expression that deaf mutes have. This expression is to be
recognised on Mlle. Zucchi's features throughout the whole performance, and this surely is the best proof of her wonderful ability
to enter into a role and sink herself completely in it."[21] A critic
writing in the same paper a few days later observed that "balletic
habits have a corrupting effect on her acting, and the wish to dis-
card them often forces her to resort to realism with the result that,
apart from many successful moments. . . she was constantly struggling between Scylla and Charybdis. It is just as irrelevant to use
balletic devices when running impetuously about the stage as it is
to employ realism in standing on a chair to see what is going on inside the church. She errs in precisely the same way when she is
thrown out of the church, expressing her vexation like a capricious
school-mistress, stamping her feet, biting her fingers and pulling at
her apron."[22]

Virginia gave her last performance of the season in the middle of February, but stayed on in St. Petersburg to see the debut of
her compatriot and fellow-pupil of Montani, Emma Bessone, in

Giselle on April 24th. She watched the performance from one of the boxes in the *bel étage*, and was recognised there during the curtain calls at the end and given a personal ovation.

The success of Virginia's second season at the Imperial Theatres was again reflected by the box-office returns. She had danced in twenty-one performances, for which the receipts had averaged 2,695 roubles. This compared with a paltry 1,375 roubles for the performances in which she did not take part. Little wonder then that before she left Russia Vsevolozhsky, Director of the Imperial Theatres, offered her a contract for the following season. She was to return on October 13th to give twelve performances for a fee of 6,000 roubles and a half benefit and was to create the leading role in a new ballet by Petipa's assistant, Lev Ivanov.

Farewell to
the Imperial Stage

Before returning to St. Petersburg for her third season at the Imperial Theatres, Virginia paid two visits to Warsaw. On June 4th, 1887, she made her first appearance at the Teatr Wielki in *La Fille mal gardée,* and in the six performances that followed presented two more of her celebrated interpretations, *Coppélia* and *Brahma.* The Polish audiences were familiar with the technical virtuosity of the Italian school, for the Warsaw ballet had been headed for the past few years by Maria Giuri, but such powerful miming from a ballerina had never been seen before. Virginia's absorption in her role was a source of astonishment. "The ballerina," noted one of the Polish critics, "did not forget her role outside the mime scenes. When Zucchi dances she is always aware of the character she is portraying. Instead of the conventional appeal, 'Look, how beautiful and graceful I am,' she seems to be asking, 'Do you understand me?' XYZ, who has been dozing for a quarter of a century in his favourite seat, is not at all pleased that the head should thus interfere with affairs of the toes, but you cannot please everybody."[1] Another critic observed that notwithstanding her short stature, she seemed to fill the stage as soon as she appeared, and varied the dynamics of her performance with infinite gradations. "Vivacious as a spark, strong, and with the tension of sprung steel, she can lull herself into calm, and swoon, and the next moment explode with a *furia italiana* blazing in her veins."[2] Her acting was so gripping that the spectators seemed to experience the emotions that she was expressing by so many delicate touches—"a slight curl of the lips, a flash of the eye, a twitch of her cheek, a flutter of the hands,

109

even her manner of holding her fingers, which play their part, together with her whole body, in a complete mime performance." So
great was her success that she was invited to return for a further
series of performance at the end of September.

Meanwhile, in St. Petersburg, the vogue for the pyrotech-
nics of the Italian school continued unabated, and that summer Italian dancers were featured at all three of the principal pleasure gardens. At Arcadia there was not only another extraordinary ballerina
in the person of Giovannina Limido, appearing in excerpts from *Excelsior* and performing "*tours de force* such as *doubles ronds de
jambe en l'air* or *pas de ciseaux*, which until now none of our ballerinas has dared attempt," but a no less remarkable male dancer,
Enrico Cecchetti, whose "interminable series of turns" revealed a
prowess that excelled that of the finest gymnasts.[3] On the Islands,
at Livadia, another new star had risen, the delightful Carlotta Brianza, for whom difficulties did not seem to exist; while at the Zoological Gardens Adelina Sozo had returned for her second season to
dance in an extravaganza called *The Last Days of Pompeii.*

As if this were not enough, there were more delights in
store for the balletomanes when the Maryinsky reopened its
doors in September. Emma Bessone was to inaugurate the season;
and Virginia, who had originally spear-headed this Italian invasion,
was to return in the middle of November and in December confront
her rival from Eden-Théâtre days, Elena Cornalba, who was then to
make her Russian debut.

Virginia arrived in St. Petersburg in time to see the first performance of *The Tulip of Harlem.* This was the new ballet by Ivanov
that she had been under contract to create, but during the summer
she had been released from this obligation to enable her to play the
part of Pepita in a revised version of *The King's Command.* It was a
happy exchange, for *The Tulip of Harlem*, in which Bessone had a
certain success, proved a disappointing work. Although it was
splendidly mounted, the action was muddled and the music poor.

The modest *Fille mal gardée*, in which Virginia made her appearance on November 16th, was a welcome contrast. After a long
series of half empty houses, the Maryinsky Theatre was again filled
to capacity. Virginia had not fully recovered from an indisposition,
but did not want to disappoint her admirers. She seemed a little
thinner, but was in good form. Her interpretation was as wonderfully original as ever, and in the *grand pas de deux* the audience thrilled
to her daring leap into the arms of Gerdt and applauded wildly
"both the variations on the *pointes*, which she did with exquisite
delicacy, and the eleven consecutive turns on the *pointe* of one
foot."[4]

Petipa's revised version of *The King's Command* was presented a few weeks later, on November 30th. The original production of
this ballet two years before had been unsatisfactory in several respects, not the least being the lack of interest in the ballerina role.
The revisions were a decided improvement, but the new version still
lacked those strong dramatic passages and love scenes in which Virginia excelled, her opportunities for interpretation hardly extending
beyond a few moments of coquetry. It was mainly in the dance content that her part had been strengthened. There was a new *pas* in
the last act, *La Gallarda*, which would have been more effective if
it had not been placed so close to the mime and dance scene of the
Charmeuse. The highlight of the production, however, was a new
pas de deux in which she was partnered by Cecchetti, who had
made his debut at the Maryinsky a few days before. Entitled *Le Pêcheur et la Perle*, it was described by the *Journal de St. Pétersbourg*
as "eminently poetic. The fisherman casts his net, a pearl is caught
in it, and this pearl is Mlle. Zucchi. He retains her in his net throughout the adagio. She then escapes to dazzle him with the most stunning arabesques, only to be finally trapped once again in the net.
M. Cecchetti himself performed a series of *entrechats* and turns
that made the public more dizzy than himself, for he finished firmly
on his legs. Mlle. Zucchi, too, after manoeuvring interminably on

the *pointe* of one foot, continues dancing on *pointe* without a break, and all with an exquisite grace."[5]

To the public it seemed so easy, but for the two dancers there was a problem to be concealed. Virginia's costume had been designed with a high Medici collar, decorated with pearls. Her remonstrances that she was in danger of entangling herself in the net were brushed aside, and the pearls were firmly sewn on. Came the first performance and, in spite of all the care the dancers took, the dreaded accident happened. Cecchetti suddenly felt a tug, and there was his ballerina caught like a fish and struggling to free herself.

"Pull, Cecchetti, pull hard!" she whispered desperately.

He did as he was told, and finally collar and pearls came away, and the pearls scattered on the stage in all directions.

When they laughed about the incident afterwards, Virginia exclaimed: "I knew it would happen. I knew it, but M. Petipa would not listen to me!"[6] *

On December 4th Emma Bessone took her farewell benefit. It was, of course, her evening, culminating with the usual ovation and presentations, but the climax was not one of her dazzling displays of virtuosity but the poetic *tableau de fantaisie* from Perrot's *La Naïade et le Pêcheur,* in which the Ondine assumes the guise of the fisherman hero to entice away her mortal rival Giannina. Bessone took the latter role, and Virginia appeared in travesty as the false fisherman. "It was a most exquisite mime scene," wrote an eye-witness, "rendered with incomparable charm and delicacy, and followed by the dazzling tarantella from *La Muette de Portici*, thrown off with true Neapolitan *furia* by the two ballerinas and the *corps de ballet.* The tarantella was encored and the two dancers, who at one moment embraced one another in the most friendly way, were recalled afterwards at least a dozen times."[7]

*When Karsavina made her formal debut at the Maryinsky on May 15th, 1902 she danced this *pas de deux* with Fokine.

Emma Bessone was followed by Virginia's old rival, Elena Cornalba, who made her Russian debut in *Fiammetta* later in December. It was not entirely her fault that the impression she made was not wholly favourable, for she did not know the ballet and had insufficient time to learn the original choreography. This was in fact no more than had happened to Virginia when she was presented with the task of learning *Daughter of Pharaoh* for her own Russian debut, but Cornalba, for all her exceptional qualities, lacked the genius of her compatriot. At her debut she managed to rouse the audience's enthusiasm by a display of speed and energy in a classical *pas de deux* with Cecchetti, but her shortcomings did not go unnoticed. The critics recognised the "minutely cultivated technique"[8] of her legs, but reproached her for her ungainly body and hands and a want of grace and elegance. Unlike the Italians who had preceded her, however, she did possess elevation, although, by the standards of the Russian dancers, not to any unusual degree. Later in the season she was to follow Bessone in the role of Emma in *The Tulip of Harlem* and to create the role of Amata in Petipa's *Vestal.*

Vsevolozhsky had now made his plans for the following season, and while adhering to the policy of engaging Italian stars—Luigia Algisi, Elena Cornalba and Carlotta Brianza were all to appear— he had decided not to renew Virginia's contract. This melancholy fact was known when she took her benefit on January 29th, 1888, and only added to the excitement of the occasion. All St. Petersburg seemed to have found its way into the theatre, and it was certainly a field day for the ticket touts. Even Virginia, with all her experience of enthusiasm, was unprepared for the storm of applause that broke out when she first came on stage in *Coppélia.* She was visibly taken aback, and those who were sitting near the stage could see the tears well up in her eyes.

Her choice of the first two acts of *Coppélia* and two scenes from *Brahma* could not have been bettered. With its powerful drama *Brahma* revived memories of that first Russian summer when she drew the young balletomanes to the theatre at Kin Grust, while *Coppélia* showed her in a new guise, that of a comedienne. St. Petersburg was already familiar with this latter ballet, which Petipa had produced, with Varvara Nikitina as Swanilda, in 1884. Virginia had developed her own interpretation of the part and did not wish to dance the variation that had been created for Nikitina. Petipa was nearly always prepared to change variations to suit ballerinas with marked individual qualities, and he readily complied with Virginia's requirements.[9]

Her original interpretation came as a surprise. No one had expected very much of *Coppélia*, looking on it as a sort of curtain-raiser to the passion that was to be unleashed in *Brahma,* and the first act struck a relatively quiet note. But in the doll scene of the second act the ballet came to life. In a costume she had designed herself, she looked the very image of a Nuremburg doll and danced the waltz with her large expressive eyes strangely immobile and her movements awkward and mechanical. "She was not afraid of being funny," noted the cirtic of *Novosti.* "She gave a complete impression of a doll, just as if she really was one. Every movement was full of observation, wit and subtle comedy, every detail thought out, every small thing wonderfully done."[10] Her performance was an inspiration to everyone on the stage, and the Russian soloists playing Swanilda's companions surprised everybody by the way in which they entered into the spirit of the comedy.

Of course, *Brahma* was what everyone was waiting for, and nobody was disappointed. Cecchetti had produced a shortened version, consisting of the second scene, for which he had arranged a new *pas d'action*, and the famous fourth scene, Virginia's "hobby-horse." In the *pas d'action* the adagio—"Cecchetti produced adagios better than anyone else," wrote Skalkovsky[11] —was a veritable drama in a nutshell. But everything paled in comparison with the famous daggers scene. Here Virginia surpassed herself in the incredible power of her performance, her emotions ranging from a gentle concern for the god she loves to the pent-up fury with which she confronts the assassins. "At times," wrote the *Journal de St. Pétersbourg*, "she reminded us, with her bristling hair and her impetuous attack, of Henri Regnault's painting of Salome."[12]

The customary presentation of gifts took place after the first act of *Coppélia*. Floral tributes were handed across the orchestra pit in all forms—sheaves, bouquets, wreaths, cornucopias—and in such profusion that they had to be carried away afterwards by the coachload. Among the more precious gifts were two superb pieces, made by the court jeweller Gau, that brought gasps of admiration from the audience: from the public, an enormous laurel wreath in silver, with a gold ribbon bearing the arms of the city in enamel and inscribed with the titles of all the ballets she had danced in on the Imperial stage, and, as a removable attachment that could be used as a brooch, her initials set in diamonds; and from the company, a large silver lyre with gold strings. It was estimated that in the history of the Russian theatre such a wealth of gifts had been matched only once before—for Adelina Patti. The great prima donna may not have been pleased had she ever learnt that her record had been equalled, for she seems to have looked on the ballet as an inferior art, and spoke slightingly of Virginia as being "tousle-haired," "bow-legged" and "a musical snuff box."[13] Virginia received no less than twenty-six curtain calls that evening, and one critic ended his notice by asking incredulously: "Is it possible that after all this enthusiasm, after these demonstrations, so beloved an artist as Virginia Zucchi will not be reengaged?"[14]

On February 15th she appeared in *Esmeralda*, and in spite of the fact that the actor Sazanov was taking his benefit and Masini was singing in *Lucrezia Borgia* the same evening, the Maryinsky was as packed as ever. At the end she was presented with a wreath inscribed "*Vedi Zucchi e puoi mori,*" (see Zucchi and die). Her last appearance at the Maryinsky, in *Coppélia* and *The King's Command*, took place on March 12th. She was to have appeared once

more, but her farewell performance was cancelled on account of
the official mourning for the German Emperor. Her admirers still
could not believe that Vsevolozhsky could be so foolish as not to
reengage the one ballerina who could draw full houses, for the sole
reason, so it was alleged, "that the Direction does not wish to yield
to the demands of the public. What if we all ignore the ballet again,
and at the debuts of Algisi and Brianza leave the theatre officials to
slumber in their seats in the wilderness which ballet will once more
produce next season?"[15] "A mediocrity such as Mlle. Brianza,"
wrote another critic, "even two such dancers, can certainly not replace Mlle. Zucchi. . . . It is often said that Russian dancers do not
draw full houses, but which of the Italians do? Only Mlle. Zucchi."[16]

The ballet season closed on March 18th with a performance
of *The Vestal* with Cornalba. Virginia had taken a box in the *bel
étage*, and in the days before the performance her faithful servitors
Skalko and Bezo—whether with her connivance history does not record—were busy paying visits to certain of the leading balletomanes.
The theatre was unusually full for a performance in which she was
not appearing, but otherwise all was normal until the curtain fell at
the end of the second act. Then, at a prearranged signal, the whole
theatre seemed to explode into applause and a procession formed,
making its way to Virginia's box. Realising that the demonstration
was for her, she stood up and began to bow her acknowledgments,
making gestures of regret that she could not go on to the stage to
thank them. Her eyes filled with tears as the ovation continued, and
her box quickly filled with bouquets and baskets of flowers. A second ovation followed at the end of the performance, with cries of
"Do not leave us! We will not let you go!"

That this was a protest against the Direction's refusal to re-
engage her did not go unperceived. Officials tried in vain to quell
the ovation. However, in Russia popular demonstrations against
authority were looked upon with grave disfavour. Whether or not

this protest was regarded in higher circles as an affront to authority, the Emperor, notwithstanding his known partiality for Virginia, made no sign that her contract should be renewed, and Vsevolozhsky remained unshaken in his resolve.

That Cornalba was reengaged for the next season and she was not must have been doubly galling to Virginia, who was human enough to derive satisfaction from being preferred to her rival for an engagement in Odessa during the summer. It was indeed believed that she took her revenge by a subtly planned intrigue. The story went that when the impresario Josef Setov approached her with an offer to dance in the newly opened City Theatre in Odessa, she demanded an enormous fee and Setov was forced, unwillingly, to turn to Cornalba. A contract was signed with her and an advance paid. Then Setov sent details of the planned repertory. Cornalba's indignation knew no bounds when she read the list of ballets—*Brahma, Esmeralda, Coppélia*, not one of which suited her talent.

"I cannot and will not agree to dance in those ballets," she expostulated.

"You have no right to refuse," pointed out Setov's agent. "You are bound by contract, and have already accepted an advance."

"*Per Bacco! Per Maria Santa!* I will not dance at all," she exclaimed.

"Then we shall claim the penalty under the contract. We will not, and indeed cannot, stage any other ballets except those on the list."

Realising that she was powerless because she had signed a contract which did not specify the ballets in which she was to appear, she changed her tone. "Can we not compromise?" she plaintively asked, not suspecting that she was falling into the trap that had been laid for her.

"On what terms do you suggest?"

"If I return the advance, will you tear up the contract?"

The agent made a pretence at demurring, but finally agreed. So the contract was annulled and Cornalba was released, unaware that all this comedy had been done in Virginia's interests. For that same evening the Divine One left St. Petersburg by the express train, having reduced her terms to a figure which Setov could afford. [17]

Preceding her, a message sped along the telegraph wires conveying instructions that she was to be met at the Main Station with a bouquet. But by a mischance the recipient of the telegram presented the bouquet to the wrong lady. He realised his mistake almost immediately, but being too much a gentleman to snatch the bouquet back, he rushed over to Virginia and in a burst of zeal seized her luggage and carried it to her carriage. Mistaking him for an unusually dressed porter, the ballerina rewarded him with a warm smile and a twenty-kopeck piece.

The public of Odessa was bewitched by Virginia's charms, and when she took her benefit in *Coppélia*, many of the Petersburg balletomanes made the journey to the Black Sea coast to see her. There were the usual tributes, but there were also protests at the manner in which she had "fleeced" the good Russian public by buying up all the tickets and opening her apartment for their resale at greatly inflated prices. A local newspaper came out with strong criticism of this procedure. Virginia was quite unrepentant. She had followed this procedure successfully and without objection in St. Petersburg, and she did not see why she should not do likewise elsewhere.

The abrupt ending of her association with the Imperial Theatres was a blow that was harder to bear because she was aware that Vsevolozhsky's decision was not motivated by artistic considerations. As Skalkovsky expressed it, "her dismissal occurred in order to give some youth who was in love with her the chance to get married."[18] Her voluptuous Italian charm, her approachability, the provoking realism of her acting, and the gossip about her love life naturally

made her the object of many amorous advances. Inevitably she had
problems in coping with these, and it was no secret that wealthy
Russian landowner had long been pressing her to marry him. His
persistence had even reached the ears of the Italian press, which had
scornfully reported the year before: "In Russia a millionaire boyar
is offering his hand to Zucchi, proclaiming her to be the very flower
of beauty, virtue and youth—she whom a Roman prince has sum-
monsed before the Courts for the restitution of a promissory note
given in a moment of abandon and elation."[19] The infatuated admirer was none other than the Prince B. Vassilchikov who had giv-
en her his family diamonds. Now impending marriage was spoken
of openly. "We are able to state," reported the paper *Novosti*,
quoting a foreign source, "that the friends of the groom are preparing an extremely original present which they intend to give to the
talented artist on the day of her wedding. This gift consists of a
silver service with wine glasses and goblets made in the shape of
dance shoes of varying sizes. Besides its direct significance, this gift
must also serve as a demonstration that the Prince's aristocratic colleagues regard such a *mésalliance* with indulgence."[20]   But his family took a different view of the matter. They made an alarmed appeal to the Tsar for his paternal protection, which was exercised
with utter disregard for the artistic and financial welfare of the
Imperial ballet.

   Virginia was greatly embarrassed by the publicity given to
the affair and, to put an end to the rumours, publicly denied reports
of her marriage in a letter to *Le Figaro*. [21] The prince, however, remained a loyal friend, and she enjoyed his protection for some
years.

   She left St. Petersburg that spring feeling bitterly aggrieved,
for she had come to think of herself as part of the Russian ballet. In
past years, when she had returned to Italy for the summer, she
would proudly extol its virtues to her countryfolk, telling them that
nowhere but in St. Petersburg was such a perfectly trained and har-

monious *corps de ballet* to be found, nor soloists who could replace a ballerina in case of emergency, and she lost no opportunity of praising the great gifts of Petipa. Now all this was to be a closed chapter in her life. It was a hard adjustment to make. "Only after her connection with the Imperial Theatres had been severed," observed Pleshcheyev, "did the imprint of grief darken her wonderful features."[22]

An Unproductive Interlude

The next two years were to be virtually unproductive, adding little
to her reputation or to her fortune. Several times more she was to
make the long journey back to Russia, but inevitably now under
less favourable conditions, with an inferior company and a limited
and almost unchanging repertory. She had to rely on a small handful of roles, to which in this period she made only one significant
addition, that of Catarina. To maintain her reputation under such
circumstances was a task that would have defeated a lesser artist.
But with Virginia, each role at each performance was a character
to be assumed afresh, and the care with which she prepared her
interpretations impressed everyone who saw her at work. It was
during these years that she was observed through the eyes of the
young Stanislavsky and of a child who was to become prima ballerina of the Bolshoi in Moscow, Adelina Giuri. Their recollections
give a revealing insight into Virginia's artistry, which shone through
the difficulties under which she was working.

Adelina Giuri was the sister of Maria Giuri and the sister-in-
law of José Mendez, ballet-master at the Teatr Wielki in Warsaw,
where Virginia gave eight performances in the summer of 1888.
Materially it was an unfortunate engagement, for it coincided with
a visit by the dramatic company of the Alexandrinsky Theatre, and
the competition was so damaging that one of her performances
grossed less than 300 roubles. For this blow to her self-esteem Virginia found consolation in the friendship of the Mendez family,
whom she persuaded to accompany her to Moscow, where she was
engaged to appear with an Italian ballet company at the Hermitage

Theatre. Mendez was to be her ballet-master, and Adelina, who was then sixteen, could not be left behind. Thus she was given the opportunity of observing Virginia Zucchi at close hand—an experience that she never forgot. Many years later she recorded in her memoirs all she could remember of two of Virginia's greatest interpretations, Lise and Padmana.

"How," she asked rhetorically, "did she attain such heights? She conveyed to the spectators simply, without any straining, and naturally what she felt herself. While preparing *La Fille mal gardée* Zucchi, who at that time was living in France, observed the popular fêtes of towns and villages (the so-called *sagres*, a type of fair-ground amusement) with their typical scenes of wooing, and prim and proud parents trying to make a good match for their daughters while the young people were having a good time among the merry village crowds. Zucchi obtained her material for *La Fille mal gardée* from the heart of popular life, and that is why she was so incomparable. . . in this ballet, where the *couleur locale* was conveyed with such absolute mastery."[1]

Some years later, in 1896, Adelina Giuri was herself to play Lise at the Moscow Bolshoi, and in a conversation with the dance historian Yuri Bakhrushin, she acknowledged that it was from Virginia Zucchi that she learnt how to interpret the part. Bakhrushin was fascinated by her account because "it was completely the Stanislavsky method. . . . In the first act Zucchi asked for what reasons she had to appear. Giuri answered that it was her music. 'That's no good,' said Zucchi and then explained, 'You know that Colas must come, you even agreed all about the ribbon. He came on time, but of course you were not ready. He knocked several times, but you were adjusting your head-dress which did not please you, then something with your skirt was not as it should have been. As for Colas, you were sure that he would wait. At last you appeared all dressed up. Nobody! Oh! he is hiding somewhere. No! He cannot have gone away! Yes, he has disappeared! His conduct is unheard of,

unpardonable. . . . And all because of this dress. . . . You see,' said
Zucchi, 'how many reasons you have for acting, all that will enrich
your image.' Giuri told me that Zucchi always paid great attention
to folk dances and studied them in all the countries she visited. Her
theory was that folk dances develop expressiveness.''[2]

The other indelible memory that the young Giuri received
from watching Virginia in action was the daggers scene in *Brahma*,
which she could see in her imagination to the end of her days in all
its vivid detail. "Brahma and his devoted Padmana, covered with a
single cloak, were walking beneath the columns of an Indian temple," she described. "Brahma lay down to rest on a marble bench
and fell asleep. Zucchi, like a small child, sat on the ground nearby,
laying her head on her arms and looking at Brahma with a gaze of
inexpressible love. At the same time five Indian priests came out of
the temple doors. Padmana sensed danger. Without making any gesture, she raised herself slightly and, slowly bending her back with
outstretched arms, she almost lay upon Brahma, shielding him from
danger. In the meantime her eyes were fixed on the faces of the
priests, who continued to approach. Moved by love, she seemed to
gather all her inner strength. Rising up, she seemed to become a
figure of Nemesis. With her inner strength expressed in her gaze and
her arms, Zucchi fearlessly approached the priests. In two gestures
she conveyed her thoughts: 'Kill him? No, never!' Making them
drop their weapons, she forced them to depart. When Brahma
awoke, her figure, her look, her back which was turned to the public—all expressed the joy of victory and unbounded love.''[3]

These memories went back to the summer of 1888 when
Virginia visited Moscow. She must have been nervous at the thought
of facing a Russian audience without the resources of the Imperial
Theatres behind her, but her apprehension was lessened by the
support of the manager of the Hermitage Theatre—her old friend,
Mikhail Lentovsky, who had presided over her first Russian triumph
at Kin Grust several years before. He was delighted to be of service

to her again and had made his preparations with typical thoroughness. His bill-stickers had covered the walls of Moscow with posters bearing the one word "Zucchi," similar posters were on display in shop windows, and a flood of visiting cards had been delivered announcing the imminent arrival of the Divine Virginia. It was the worst time of year to fill a theatre in Moscow, for fashionable society had deserted the city to enjoy the summer in the country; but Virginia's fame was enough to tempt many balletomanes from their country retreats to attend her first performance, on July 17th, in *Brahma*, which Vittorio Natta, who was also her partner, had produced for her.

To judge from the reports of that evening, no one was disappointed. Not for a long time had a Moscow audience been so carried away. That the occasion should be a ballet performance was even more extraordinary, for interest in ballet had been flagging in Moscow for some years. It was significant, therefore, in more ways than one that Virginia's interpretation evoked not memories of the golden past of ballet, but the genius of the greatest artists of the dramatic stage. "It was quite extraordinary," wrote one Moscow critic, "to see how the acting of the great artist affected the public, and to gauge the artistic effect she created from the opinions, gossip and arguments that were to be heard during the intervals. It was something we have experienced only at performances of those giants of the theatre who have appeared here in recent times—Ristori, Sarah Bernhardt, Salvini, Rossi, Barnay or Possard—and it was even more wonderful when one recalls that it was a performance of a ballerina and her talent as a mime speaking without words to the soul and intellect of the public."[4]

There was not an empty seat to be seen at any of her six performances of *Brahma*. She aroused the enthusiasm even of the hardened balletomanes who cherished fond memories of the popular Praskovia Lebedeva, a ballerina of rare expressive gifts who had retired at the peak of her powers more than twenty years before.

"The old Moscow balletomanes are melting," reported *Novosti*, "and equate Zucchi with the unforgettable P. Lebedeva, who would have made a first-class mime if in her day ballerinas had not been expected to dance, dance, and dance again."[5] Virginia reminded them of Lebedeva most of all in the daggers scene, for Lebedeva had performed a somewhat similar scene in *The Corsair*, though making her impression by the expressive plasticity of her gestures, while with Virginia it was the mobility of her features that remained in the memory.

Zucchi's next role at the Hermitage was that of Lise in *La Fille mal gardée*, which was produced for her by Mendez. The ballet was presented at her benefit performance, and although she was the centre of attention, the vitality of Mendez's production was recognised and he was called before the footlights. By nature a retiring man, he had to be dragged reluctantly from the wings to be presented with a gaily painted scroll before disappearing with an embarrassed bow.

Virginia's farewell performance shortly afterwards, in which she appeared in extracts from *Brahma, La Fille mal gardée* and *Esmeralda*, set the seal on her triumph. The enthusiasm she had aroused on her arrival had been maintained to the end, and several prominent Muscovites had not missed a single performance. Many of the older balletomanes were in their seventh heaven, and one of them lent her the most precious item from his collection—the tambourine which Ekaterina Sankovskaya had used when she danced in *Esmeralda* in 1851— to use on this occasion. The excitement mounted when the time came for the gifts and the curtain calls, and there was an unexpected surprise for the audience when photographs of the ballerina were distributed among them as her farewell gift.

Virginia's fame lingered on in Moscow for some time after she had taken the train to carry her back, through Smolensk and Brest-Litovsk, to the West. If one could no longer savour the real thing, the clown Vladimir Durov substituted for her with a well-observed imitation. Wearing a ridiculous ballet costume and a tousled black wig, he gave a bustling parody of her in *Brahma,* which Virginia herself had gone to see before she left. She had laughed heartily, but it was reported that there were some who were aghast at such blasphemy!

Her destination had been Vienna, where she gave three guest performances at the Court Opera at the end of August. Because she appeared in two roles in the current repertory—Satanella in the ballet of the same name and Swanilda in *Coppélia*—her talents could be compared with those of the resident ballerina, Luigia Cerale. Cerale, who was ten years younger, was considered to have a stronger technique and greater stamina as a dancer, but there was no question of Virginia's superiority as a mime. Working in her shadow on only three nights, the Viennese dancers perceived and appreciated her unique gift, and before she left a deputation from the company called at her dwelling to present a silver laurel wreath inscribed with their names.

As winter approached, the news broke that the Divine Virginia was making plans to return to Moscow. She was gathering a large company and was to bring a vast quantity of scenery, properties and costumes which it was estimated would take several days to clear customs. José Mendez was again to be ballet-master, and Vittorio Natta the principal male dancer. The company consisted of eight soloists from the Scala, Milan, several mimes of both sexes, and a *corps de ballet* of forty-four women and twenty-four men. With a repertory consisting of *Catarina, Esmeralda* and *Brahma,* it promised to be an exciting season, and connoisseurs predicted, somewhat recklessly, that the Italian company would offer strong competition to the ballet at the Bolshoi Theatre, whose repertory one critic decried as "quite decrepit."[6]

The opening night, on November 28th, 1888, was a splendid success. The owner of the theatre, Rodon, had increased his prices to cover the heavy expenses of the season, but this had not deterred the wealthier theatregoers, whose ranks were swollen by a number of admirers from Petersburg. Also in the audience was Carlotta Brianza, who was then appearing in Moscow at the Bolshoi. Only in the gallery were empty seats to be seen: the prices there, it seemed, had been pitched above the means of the humble enthusiast.

Catarina was a colourful ballet originally produced by Jules Perrot for the Danish ballerina Lucile Grahn in 1846. Its story told of an imaginary incident in the life of the painter Salvator Rosa. While painting in the Apennine hills he falls into the hands of bandits, who are led by Catarina, the daughter of their former chief. They are attacked by soldiers: Salvator is wounded, and the bandits are captured, except for Catarina and her lieutenant Diavolino, who make their escape. By chance the soldiers, with their prisoners, stop at an inn where Catarina has taken shelter. In a dramatic scene Catarina distracts the guards by her dancing and enables the bandits to be freed. Later in the ballet Catarina is arrested and sentenced to death. In the condemned cell she is visited by a monk, who reveals himself as Salvator and helps her to escape. The ballet ended with a brilliant scene of the Roman carnival, where Catarina seeks Salvator to warn him that Diavolino has sworn to kill him out of jealousy. The three come together, and Diavolino, thrusting at his rival, kills Catarina as she interposes herself between the two men. This tragic ending had been considered too harrowing by the Imperial Theatres, where it had been replaced by a weaker *dénouement* in which the police intervene, Catarina is pardoned and Diavolino makes his escape among the revellers. Virginia, however, restored the original tragic ending, but with new music composed by the conductor of her orchestra, Signor Brancane.

Her interpretation of the title role was highly expressive, and she took full advantage of the dramatic opportunities. The scene where she charms the soldiers created a great effect, but the highlight was the death scene. One critic described it in great detail.

"The face of the artist is transformed," he wrote, "You see before
your eyes a doomed person. With death in her eyes, she raises herself slightly from the gound as if to reconcile herself with Heaven.
Desiring to atone for the sins of her lifetime, the dying Catarina
wishes to join the hands of her beloved and his betrothed. At that
moment the last spark of life flashes out with renewed strength,
and with a feeble frenzy she once more joins the hands of the two
lovers. Then death snuffs out this final spark, and Catarina, her face
infused with the great mystery of death, is about to sink into Rosa's
arms when she remembers that the bandit who has accidentally
struck her down has for all that loved her selflessly. As though wishing to forgive him for what has happened, she takes a few faltering
steps towards her killer and dies in his arms. In the final moment
she is no longer the passionate and impetuous Catarina, but a Catarina who is not of this world, a soul that has cast off all that is
earthly, that seeks heavenly forgiveness and is itself forgiving. All
this was communicated with such beautiful artistry that I could
have forgiven Zucchi anything, and my mind was filled with just
one thought: that such aesthetic enjoyment could be conveyed only
by a supremely talented artist. The pallor of death can be assumed
only by an artist who possesses the strong brilliant flame that is the
gift of God."[7]

The strength of Mendez's production of *Catarina* lay prima-
rily in his ensembles and ballabiles, but he had included some original effects. One of these came at the end of the *danse des fusils* in
the first act, when the bandit women dash forward to the footlights,
brandishing their rifles and crying *"Viva!"* Its taste, in the context of
a ballet, may have been questionable, but it contained an element of
surprise and evoked a spontaneous burst of applause. The combination of Virginia's performance, the fresh scenery and the *corps de
ballet*'s revealing costumes ("costumes such as one does not often
meet"[8]) compensated for the lack of cohesion in the company and
earned a long sequence of curtain calls for the ballerina, her ballet-
master and her partner.

Unfortunately the impetus of this first evening was not maintained. Receipts fell, and the prices had to be lowered. The second production, *Brahma*, did not succeed in rekindling the public's interest. To add to the difficulties, some of the scenery had not reached Moscow, and it had to be presented with scenery taken from the Rodon Theatre's stock, augmented by some from a private opera company. Whether the cause was nerves or the uneven stage, both Virginia and Natta fell during performances. Virginia seemed particularly depressed, and the playwright Tchekhov, who saw her in December, described her as tired.

The rot was stopped by *Esmeralda*, which at last drew a full house. This too had to be staged with a heterogeneous collection of stock scenery, but its intrinsic strength overcame this disadvantage. The public came to see Virginia in one of her greatest interpretations, which, on the evidence of one critic, seemed to grow more and more realistic with the passing of time. "The melodramatic acting of the ballerina, which depicted all too visually the torture and the anguish endured by the gypsy girl in prison before she is to be executed, had its effect on the public," he reported, "But is it artistically necessary in ballet go go to such lengths as painting the hands red to represent blood-stains and holding them in such a way as to show them broken and twisted by the rack and other tortures?"[9]

Mendez's production departed from the original scenario in the final *dénouement*. Instead of Esmeralda being led to the scaffold, Phoebus rescues her and exposes Claude Frollo, who is stabbed to death by Quasimodo. Then came the *fête des fous*, and the curtain fell with Esmeralda raising her hands in a final gesture. It might have been taken as symbolic of the extent to which the production had been focussed on her own performance, for the supporting roles were inadequately played. Mendez himself played the part of Quasimodo, but was not very convincing in his attempt to represent a hunchback.

Virginia would have welcomed the presence of a real hunchback, as her friend Constantin Stanislavsky discovered. During her

stay in Moscow she was a welcome visitor at the home of the Sta-
nislavskys, where a small private theatre had been installed for the
pleasure of the family. Constantin and his brothers were determined
that she should dance on their stage, and they eventually achieved
this through a clever stratagem. In their household was a tutor who
was a hunchback, and discovering that their superstitious guest considered it lucky to kiss a hunchback a certain number of times,
they planned a production of *Esmeralda*, in which the tutor was
cast as Quasimodo. Virginia readily fell in with the idea, grasping at
the opportunity to play Esmeralda with a real hunchback, whom
the action required her to kiss. The rehearsals that followed gave
great pleasure as an after-dinner diversion, but they also proved a
penetrating experience for Constantin Stanislavsky, who though
still in his mid-twenties was already beginning to form his theories
of production that were to have such a potent effect on the theatre
in later years.

Persuaded both to produce the work and to play the part of
Esmeralda, Virginia undertook the task as seriously as if she had
been working for the Imperial Theatres. For the young Stanislavsky
it was an object lesson to watch her moulding her role with
the object of making the hunchback believe her. "She was
first of all a dramatic actress," recalled Stanislavsky in his memoirs,
"and only after that a dancer, although she was a great dancer also.
I saw at these foolish rehearsals her limitless imagination, her ferti-
lity of combination, her originality, her taste in the choice of new
stage problems and stage business, her unusual experience, and most
of all a näive, childish faith in what she was doing at the moment
and what was taking place around her. She gave this all of her attention whole-heartedly and completely. She seemed to pour her own
desires into the souls of her actors, like a hypnotist who enters into
the soul of his subject."

What struck Stanislavsky above all else was "the softness of
her muscles in moments of great spiritual stress in the drama that

took place in the ballet, when I touched her in order to support her as her dancing partner."[10] This experience revealed to him his own shortcomings as a performer. He realised that he was much too concerned with imitating others instead of relying on his own taste and originality and that this produced both physical and spiritual strain. This was the great lesson he learnt from Virginia Zucchi.

Her friendship with Stanislavsky was some compensation for the disappointing results of her season at the Rodon Theatre. Ill luck had played its part in this, but Virginia's inexperience as an impresario had been revealed in the overcharging, and there were complaints about the indecency of the costumes worn by the *corps de ballet* and, in some instances, by Virginia herself. She was now to return to St. Petersburg, and the Muscovites wondered how the ladies of the Imperial capital would react to the taste of the Italian dancers.

Early in the New Year of 1889 Virginia Zucchi, with her horde of dancers and musicians and all their scenery, costumes, properties, instruments and music, arrived in St. Petersburg. There she was soon brought face to face with reality, for the Nemetti Theatre in Ofitserskaya Street was small and ugly and had none of the grand atmosphere to which she had been accustomed at the Maryinsky. For the public there was an added disillusionment in the inadequate standards of her dancers, which threw the performances into still greater contrast with her earlier triumphs on the Imperial stage. But as the season got under way, it was clear that she had lost little of her personal magnetism, and her young admirers were moved to lay their coats on the pavement for her to walk on to her carriage after her first performance. One of these was Alexandre Benois, who, while taking part in this symbolic gesture, was cold at heart. That same evening he vowed to keep his memory of her untarnished, and he never saw her dance again.

The season opened on January 23rd with *Brahma*. It was
the first time that this ballet had been given in Russia in its entirety,
although it was already well known from the abridged version that
Virginia had brought to St. Petersburg in 1885. The daggers scene
was almost inseparably associated with her histrionic genius, but of
late it had become almost too familiar, for Raoul Gunsbourg had
been giving a hilarious imitation of it in a revue at Arcadia. But the
intensity and truth of Virginia's acting quickly overcame any impi-
ous memories and, although she had lost the fresh bloom of youth,
she was wildly applauded, first in *Brahma*, and later in *La Fille mal
gardée, Esmeralda* and *Catarina.*

During her seasons at the Imperial Theatres she had repeat-
edly asked for *Catarina* to be revived for her, but to no avail, and it
was galling that it should have been staged at the Maryinsky a few
months before for the inexperienced Luigia Algisi. As might have
been foreseen, Algisi made little impression, and on February 15th
the Nemetti Theatre was packed to see Virginia play the role of
Catarina for the first time in St. Petersburg. The excitement was
intense. One old balletomane, whose experience went back to the
time of Taglioni, declared that as an actress she could only be compared with Rachel and Ristori. She rendered Catarina as a spirited
girl, courageous, passionate and deeply in love. It was a true study
of character, full of original and subtle nuances. In the dance in
which Catarina charms the guards, she infused a sentimental touch
that softened her ardent show of temperament. And in the prison
scene, when Salvator appears to Catarina after she has lost all hope,
she avoided the obvious reaction. "Instead of the consternation
and reckless happiness that one might have expected," noted one
critic, "Zucchi's Catarina expresses a complete mistrust of what
she sees with her own eyes, and only after much hesitation and in-
decision does she dare believe in her unexpected happiness, which
she expresses with impetuous and passionate caresses."[11]

Her performances drew packed houses to the Nemetti, but
on the alternate evenings, which were devoted to a French light

opera company, the theatre was virtually deserted. At the end of January the unfortunate singers had to admit disaster and insolvency, and to aid the stranded artists, a benefit performance was organised in which both Virginia and her compatriot, the tenor Angelo Masini, gave their services. As a consequence of the singers' departure Virginia appeared every night in the last weeks of the season, and at the end gave matinées as well as evening performances. Elated by the enthusiastic response of the public, she seemed indefatigable. Writing of this season, Skalkovsky recorded that she was heavier, but still danced "creditably" in *grands pas de deux* and rendered an oriental dance called *La Mongolienne* "with much passion and sweetness." He also mentioned a variation on the *pointes*, containing some taxing *petite batterie,* that she danced "not badly" to the melody of the *Berliner Polka.*[12]

At her benefit performance she gave an impressive display of versatility, appearing in excerpts from *Catarina, Coppélia* and *La Fille mal gardée* and the scene from *La Naïade et le Pêcheur.* In the space of a few hours she covered a vast range of interpretation, from the comedy of *Coppélia* to the spine-chilling tragedy of *Catarina,* and from the rustic charm of *La Fille mal gardée* to the travesty role of the disguised naiad. The audience sensed the unique nature of the occasion. At her first entrance in *Coppélia* the applause was so prolonged that the orchestra had to stop playing. There were twenty-four curtain calls at the end, and gifts in such profusion—many of them, it was noted, from the ladies of St. Petersburg—that she had to be lifted over them to come forward to take her bow. Among the wreaths was one with an inscription that everyone understood as a reproof to the Imperial Theatres: "What we possess we do not keep."

The hint was not taken: there was no approach from the Imperial Theatres, where Vsevolozhsky and Petipa were occupied with the preparations for *The Sleeping Beauty*. Virginia would have given much to have danced at the Maryinsky again, but powerful forces were at work to keep her out. She was well accustomed to intrigue and, while she knew when to ignore malicious gossip, she had an intuition that warned her to be vigilant. There was in fact an incident during this season which could have had serious consequences for her. In one of her ballets she had to climb a ladder to make an appearance high above the stage. Although this could have been done by an understudy, it was her practice to ascend the ladder herself. One evening, however, she had a premonition and asked her understudy to take her place. The understudy did so, but when the time came to descend, the ladder had been removed.

After their last performance on March 2nd, the company packed its baggage and departed on a tour of the Baltic States. Wherever they appeared—Riga, Mitau, Libau, Vilno—they found enthusiastic audiences, but the financial burden of the enterprise was crippling, and Virginia was glad to be able to close the accounts and return, alone, to St. Petersburg, to be engaged at the risk and peril of an impresario.

Her new impresario was none other than the Raoul Gunsbourg whose impersonation of her had been the talk of St. Petersburg. A more original character it would have been hard to imagine. At that time he had barely crossed the threshold of a career in the theatre that was to stretch to the eve of the Second World War, but already at the age of thirty he had a wealth of experience behind him. Brought up in a strict Jewish Orthodox family in Bucharest, he had seen some adventurous service in the Russo-Turkish War of 1878 and had later made his way across Europe to St. Petersburg, where he very quickly found his feet in the theatre, first as a comedian and then as a manager. His wartime deeds had brought him to the notice of the Imperial family, and he had been appointed to direct the performances at Peterhof and Krasnoye Selo.

In appearance this remarkable young man cut a striking figure: small of stature, clean-shaven, with curly hair and firmly moulded features that set one seeking for a well-known resemblance. To one his mischievous expression would recall the face of

Voltaire, while another was reminded of the young Beethoven. His features, and indeed his whole body, seemed to be constantly in motion: "to see him," wrote the French critic, Fourcaud, "you feel he is living by his nerves and his will power."[13] Most people with whom he came in contact found him irresistible. His fund of anecdotes was apparently inexhaustible, and his gift for mimicry quite uncanny. Virginia was not his only victim, for he gave impressions of Sarah Bernhardt, Anna Judic and other actresses, that were equally true to life; but his most comical turn was a demonstration of a man and a woman taking their bath.

The summer of 1889 found Gunsbourg directing the Arcadia pleasure gardens, where he had assembled a distinguished company of singers from the Paris Opéra, Covent Garden and the Brussels Monnaie, whom he had reinforced with two military bands, clowns and acrobats, and a ballet company that was to be headed by Virginia for the first two months of the season.

The dancers and the orchestra were no more than adequate, but this did not dim Virginia's triumph in *Esmeralda* in which she opened on May 23rd. Just as Johann Strauss is the King of the waltz, wrote Veto in *Novosti*, so Virginia Zucchi is the Queen of mime. Seeing her, one forgot everything else: "Zucchi is everywhere—like a precious painting by a great master, the qualities of which are independent of the limitations of its surroundings."[14] The great moments were untarnished: the scene at the betrothal party had lost none of its effect, and the last act seemed more harrowing than ever. Some critics, however, reproved her for an excessive realism in representing the effects of torture. "Her movements, admirably observed though they are, overstep the limits required by aesthetics," wrote one of them, "and as for the bloodstains left on her neck and arms by the instruments of torture, they remind us too much of those wax figures in anatomical museums for us to approve of them on the stage. Moreover, a talent such as Mlle. Zucchi's has no need of such 'refinements' to make an impression. She did not resort to them, if we remember rightly, at the Maryinsky Theatre, and yet her acting there was most effective."[15]

In the weeks that followed she appeared in *Brahma, La Fille mal gardée* and *Catarina*, and was joined by a new partner, Victor Gillert. The audiences at Arcadia were generally easy to please, but one evening, in *Brahma*, she made a significant conquest. The celebrated music critic, Vladimir Stasov, who did not care for the ballet, found himself gripped by the drama and afterwards wrote to his friend Ilya Repin, the painter: "It is really worth seeing. I even recommend it to you. Zucchi is *very talented*, not for the absurd ballet dancing which I cannot stand, but for her magnificent miming."[16]

The season's only novelty was Virginia's own production of *Sieba*. With the limited resources at her disposal, it was inevitably a modest production, even in comparison with Cecchetti's staging of it for Limido at Arcadia in 1887. But if there was little left of Manzotti's famous *ensembles*, Virginia's own performance was what people paid to see. For the role of the Scandinavian goddess she wore a blonde wig that was very becoming and strangely smooth and untousled. Ably supported by Gillert, she displayed "her sense of plastique, her firm balance and her vivacity" in the *pas de deux*, and if her *pointe* work lacked the brilliance of Limido's, her miming was without question vastly superior. The audience shared Sieba's anguished situation when she was smitten with love for the king, and in the celebrated underworld scene, which had to be much curtailed, Virginia gave "a perfect rendering of a soul in torment, vaporous and light, as she springs in the air, struggling against the evil spirits."[17] Skalkovsky, who knew her so well, detected a sense of melancholy in this performance which he attributed to the financial losses she had incurred as her own impresario.

The ballet was first given at her benefit performance, during which she publicly received offerings of flowers and many valuable gifts. Among these was a diadem with five diamond stars, and a gift

that caused a certain amount of puzzlement—a silver wash-stand.
"Some people," commented Skalkovsky, remembering no doubt
how, in her first summer in Russia, soap had seemed a rather precious commodity, "took this as being rather ironical."[18]

Arcadia was a far cry from the splendours of the Imperial
Theatres, and at times Virginia had to stretch her ingenuity to the
limit to obtain the effect she desired. There was one occasion when
the right costume could not be found and she draped herself in a
sheet, which she gathered around her waist with a length of string
so skilfully that from the front of the house she appeared beautifully dressed. But these conditions seemed in no way to affect her
power of attraction. People came great distances to see her, not only from Pavlovsk, Peterhof and other towns that were reasonably
accessible, but even from as far afield as Moscow. One Moscow bus-
inessman did not miss a performance, spending most of his time in
the train shuttling between the two cities. On each visit he would
send her a bouquet and a suckling pig in aspic, a delicacy of which
she became specially fond, but he never ventured to present himself
to her. When someone asked the motive for such assiduous attendance, he confessed that he thought little of Virginia's dancing and
found the *corps de ballet* terrible, but that he would make the journey to see her miming even if he had to come from Siberia.

It was plain to see that the fears expressed in Moscow that
she might shock the ladies of St. Petersburg were unfounded.
Whether or not the latter were more tolerant in their taste where
theatrical costume was concerned, the majority of her admirers at
Arcadia seemed to be ladies, many of whom carried their devotion
to the point of wearing their hair *à la Brahma*—presumably with
the aid of George Pedder's setting that was specially designed to
keep the hair tousled!

When the season ended in July, a critic writing under the
pseudonym of Veto summed up the contribution which Virginia
had made to ballet in Russia. Before her arrival in 1885, as he re-

minded his readers, ballet had been confined to the Imperial Theatres where, brilliantly staged and performed though it was, it held
little interest for the general public. The art of ballet had appealed
mainly to an exclusive set of balletomanes who assumed a sort of
proprietary interest and whose interest was in many cases centered
on the young female body. The theatre was seldom very full, the
general public being attracted chiefly by the spectacular production, to judge by the number of children who filled the boxes. All
this changed with the arrival of Virginia Zucchi. At the contact
with her dramatic miming, the like of which had not been seen before, the public's attitude changed virtually overnight. Now people
who had formerly been indifferent to the ballet came, not to be
dazzled by its spectacle, but to be moved by the interpretative art
of the ballerina. This was a revolutionary change, for which
Virginia was alone responsible, for the Italian dancers who followed
her were not mimes, but virtuoso technicians. "Of course," the critic went on, "she needed a large stage and a splendid production,
but perhaps ballets would have been created for her in which grace
and plastique without technical virtuosity, and above all miming,
would have been dominant. The term 'tragedienne of mime' con-
veys the essence of Zucchi's talent, and the opinion of an admirer
of Shakespeare's *Hamlet* that Zucchi would be capable of conveying the celebrated 'To be or not to be' soliliquy can be understood
when you see her acting in her finest roles."[19]

The Riviera and Bayreuth

As her dancing career moved inevitably to its close, Virginia Zucchi felt more and more drawn to the property she owned at Cortemaggiore. Here, each summer, she snatched a few happy weeks, revelling in the peace of the Lombardy plain. Here she found not only the repose she needed after an exhausting round of performances but a spiritual refreshment that few of her worldly admirers would have easily understood. "She was born for quiet, she longed for tranquillity," explained Ugo Capetti, who knew her well. "For her the stage is only a life of passage. She loves the gentleness of the countryside, and the serene resignation of its life. While the world talks about the star spoilt by her proud climb to fame, while the public clamours to see her over and over again on the stage, while people chatter about the good fortune that rains on ladies of the theatre, she returns to her gentle dream of being a quiet countrywoman; she gazes on the friendly landscape, she listens to the songs of the poultry yard, dreams of the dancing of swallows, and declares, that Désireé in Zola's *La Faute de l'Abbé Mouret* is her ideal."[1]

It was typical of her simple, uncomplicated nature that she should identify herself, not with the passionate child of nature who, in the novel, stirs the dormant senses of the priestly hero, but with his sister, who communes with the birds and animals in the presbytery back yard and is left untouched by the soul-searing experience that befalls her brother.

For the moment these bucolic delights had to be savoured in moderation for, although she had passed her fortieth birthday, she felt she still had more to give to the public; and there was the added problem that the expenses she had incurred, and was still to incur, as her own impresario, made it difficult to contemplate an early retirement. Now, for the first time in five years, there was no engagement to take her back to Russia, and she was forced to make arrangements to pass the winter nearer at hand. Seeing no hope of being engaged at the Scala, she once again assembled a company, with the experienced Cesare Marzagora as ballet-master and Giovanni Carbone as principal male dancer, and signed a contract to give a short season at the Teatro Dal Verme in Milan in October 1889.

The choice of *Coppélia* as the opening work might have seemed a sure guarantee of success, but Virginia had counted without the conditioning of the Milanese public by the grand historical and melodramatic epics of Italian choreography and more recently by the modern spectacles of Manzotti. In comparison with these weighty works, *Coppélia* with its artless charm left the audience puzzled. The first act was punctuated by rumblings of discontent and protest, which subsided only when she was on the stage, but in the second act the performance came suddenly to life. She saved the day single-handed with the doll scene, which she gave with such a fine feeling for comedy that what from another dancer might have appeared vulgar became, in her hands, a display of delicate elegance. "We have here not a ballerina," wrote one critic, "but an actress of genius who grasps and renders a situation, a character, a whimsy, with the most exquisite interpretation."[2] *Esmeralda* and *Brahma*, which completed the repertory for the season, were more to the public's taste, and she obtained a splendid triumph with her daggers scene which moved one critic to hail her as "the Duse of ballerinas."[3]

The extraordinary power of her acting won her new admirers at every performance. Typical of these was the young playwright, Marco Praga, who had applauded her earlier at the Scala but

had not been specially impressed, but was now so enthralled that he
was in the theatre nearly every night of this season. To his expert
eye she was a unique artist—"a great actress whom chance had
made into a ballerina." He marvelled at her complete absorption in
the character she was portraying and the breadth and depth of
meaning she conveyed in her mime. "Her face is transfigured, her
eyes shine like lanterns, her features acquire an astonishing nobility,
her entire action is a marvel of finesse and emphasis," he wrote.
"She enters completely into her part, she feels and experiences everything she has to express, and she expresses it with an effectiveness
and a power that is perhaps to be found in only one actress on our
modern stage—Eleanora Duse.

"Have you seen her in *Brahma*?," he went on. "In that
little scene in the second act when the rejected God goes to buy her
as his slave, and she pours him a drink and with ingenuous coquetry displays her graces, and then, flattered by his compliments,
blushes and turns away. And in the daggers scene when, having driv-
en away the four white-bearded assassins, she is seized with an impulse of joy, a tremor that fills her whole body, and shakes her
lustrous head, looking up to the sky with eyes shining with happiness, in an *enivrement* of her whole person that is a stroke of genius.
And in the final scene, when at the sight of her loved one on the
pyre that is already smouldering, she begs forgiveness and grace from
each of the three pink-robed high priests in turn, dragging herself
along the ground in a mounting expression of grief—and they remain impassive and reject her with scorn—and then she sees the light
and, realising that all is possible, drags herself to her lover and,
clutching his garment, pulls herself up and looks at him with mingled
terror and compassion, as though to say, 'Look at me, look at me,
and have courage!'"[4]

Other evenings brought other emotions: tears springing to
the eyes at the sight of Esmeralda's anguish when being led to the
scaffold, and a quickening of the heart when she pleads forgiveness

of Phoebus, whom she believes to be killed; and in *La Fille mal gar-dée,* unrestrained laughter at the pranks of Lise as she tries to conceal Colas from her watchful mother. All the time Praga, whose vocation was the writing of dialogue, missed the melody of the voice, and in his seat at the Dal Verme he conceived a plan to hear her speak on stage. He had no difficulty in obtaining an introduction, and he boldly launched into his proposal.

"You ought to recite," he said.

At this blunt statement Virginia looked at him in amazement.

"Are you joking?" she asked.

"But no, I am serious."

She allowed herself to explore the possibility of Praga's idea, and he suggested a recital consisting of extracts from comedy and drama, to be given perhaps for charity so that the experiment should not assume the proportions of a testing ordeal. But the calls of Virginia's career cut short their discussions and the proposal languished—forgotten perhaps by the ballerina, but not by Praga, who for some years cherished the hope that it might one day be realised.

The Dal Verme season was the prelude to a visit to Nice, where Virginia and her company arrived in the middle of November in response to a summons from her old friend, Raoul Gunsbourg, who was directing the Grand Théâtre there. Nice was then a small, select resort where royalty, the cream of society and the very wealthy gathered to pass the winter: a comfortably intimate haven where the local newspaper could report as an item of interest that a visitor recently knocked down by a zealous bicyclist had been seen walking in the town, happily suffering from no ill effects. In Gunsbourg's own words it was "a little refuge of art and poetry. . . beauty's capital. . . the residence of all the Old World and the New possessed that was glorious and noble. . . . Its inhabitants represented a large part of the world's culture, art, poetry, society and

beauty. Away from the port district one or two streets were popu-
lated; the rest was nut gardens and villages. A night at the Opera of
Nice was a splendid occasion: the most beautiful women in the
most sumptuous toilettes filled the boxes of the theatre, which was
always lit *a giorno*. One could give a name to every member of the
audience, for each of them represented a cell of this little paradise."[5]

Gunsbourg found himself a sort of master of ceremonies
during the two seasons that he directed the Grand Théâtre in Nice.
So successfully did he acquit himself of his task that he quickly became one of the town's most popular characters. No one thought
it in any way inappropriate when he dressed up as Napoleon and
marched up the Promenade des Anglais as the head of an historical
procession he organised during Carnival, to be acclaimed with cries
of "Vive Gunsbourg!" To Virginia he was still the same irrepressible
friend of old, a raconteur without peer and a man with a vast web
of contacts that, joined to his bold and imaginative flair and his irresistible personality, made him a truly great impresario.

His touch was most evident in the arrangements for her
opening performance. Many visitors from St. Petersburg were in the
audience to see her in *Esmeralda*, but her greatest pleasure that evening was to see the Grand Duke Vladimir in the principal box. At
the end of the performance she was wildly cheered and deluged
with flowers. It was quite like old times. As the season progressed,
she was seen in other ballets: *Brahma, La Fille mal gardée, Catarina,*
the doll scene from *Coppélia* (given under the title *L'Illusion*) and
a new ballet called *Graziella* in which, as the local critic described
it, "there is a boa constrictor, a gentleman who looks uncannily
like François Ier, Italian girls dancing the tarantella, ondines sleeping or leaping over green gauze waves and finally Zucchi, who
becomes more and more marvellous and stupendous."[6]

The season's highlight was a production of Glinka's opera
A Life for the Tsar in January 1890. It contained, as the critic
Francisque Sarcey recorded, "some Polish dances in the second act,

a *cracovienne* and specially a mazurka, which La Zucchi led with
such dazzling brio that it was furiously encored. She graciously performed it a second time with the same verve as before, heading a
squadron of male dancers who beat out the rhythm with the heels
of their boots as they ran behind her. She possesses much animation and *entrain*, and the charm of her dancing lies in the enjoyment that she breathes into it."[7]

In the last important production of the season, *La Muette
de Portici*, Virginia obtained a great triumph in the mime role of
Fenella. The public flocked to see her in such numbers that on one
occasion more than four hundred people had to be turned away
from the theatre.

With the coming of spring Virginia made her way back to
Italy, giving performances at the Politeama Margherita in Genoa
and the Teatro Quirino in Rome before seeking the calm of Cortemaggiore. The exigences of performing and the responsibilities of
running her own company had taken their toll, and she was in real
need of a holiday. It was at Genoa that the Russian historian, Sergei
Khudekov, chanced to see her—and on an evening, as ill luck would
have it, when she was not at her best. "It was sad," he wrote, "to
see this artist, who was putting on weight and approaching fifty,*
earning a crust of bread by the sweat of her brow. Her thin dancing
was greeted with thin applause. Of Zucchi's former passion on the
stage there was no trace. Her fame lay behind her."[8] It was a harsh
judgment, but honest no doubt by the standards of the particular
performance, and not without truth. For now she was relying more
and more on qualities of interpretation to beguile the public. A
local critic who also saw her in Genoa on this visit received a very
different impression, probably because he was less aware of the
finer points of technique than Khudekov. She revealed to him, he
confessed, the secret of the furore that Taglioni and Cerrito had
created in days gone by. "Dancers no longer dance as they did,"
he went on. "But as for dancing, Zucchi does not dance, she 'em-

*She was, of course, only forty-three.

broiders.' It is not a matter of *pointes*, nor even of the legs. It is
something quite otherwise. From a look that can be as sharp as a
knife and as caressing as the kiss of a girl in love, to the movements
of a tigress defending her cubs, to the precocious abandon and voluptuous movements of a Circassian or a Gipsy, everything about
her transcends art—it is Nature itself."[9]

Virginia herself was fully aware that her stamina and
strength were on the wane and adjusted the choreography of her
roles accordingly, cutting a difficulty here, simplifying a passage
there, and generally exercising her craft to conceal her shortcomings. There were occasions, for example, when she realised she
could not bring a *manege* to a brilliant finish. Then she might flick
loose her shoulder-strap, allowing her breast to escape from her
corsage, and after giving a tantalising glimpse would finish with
her arms demurely crossed in front of her. It all happened so quickly that only the most knowledgeable recognised it as a cunning
device to distract attention from her technical inadequacy. She was
also careful not to repeat this trick too often.

A few weeks at Cortemaggiore in the summer restored her
energies, and the autumn of 1890 found her back in Milan, assem-
bling a company to take to the Anfiteatro Mangano in Palermo at
the end of the year. The repertory consisted of her usual ballets
with one notable addition, Manzotti's *Pietro Micca*. This was one
of the choreographer's early works, a ballet based on a heroic episode in the history of Italian arms. In the political climate of the
late nineteenth century, when the triumph of the Risorgimento
was still fresh in the memory, it made an immediate appeal to the
spirit of national identification. In the spring of 1891 Virginia
brought the production to Rome, at the Teatro Quirino, and Milan,
at the Dal Verme, where her performance of the mime part of
Maria, Micca's wife, was acclaimed as "one of those creations that
will pass into legend."[10]

To a foreigner, however, the patriotic spectacle appeared
absurd, and the young French writer, Romain Rolland, who saw

one of the performances in Rome, found the experience disconcerting. He had gone out of curiosity, for Zucchi's name seemed
to be on everyone's lips in Roman society, and so strange was the
form of ballet that he saw that it was not easy for him to arrive at
a fair appraisal of her talent. He wrote of his experience to his
mother, and his letter is doubly interesting for in addition to his
opinion of Virginia, he gave a revealing account of an Italian ballet
as it appeared to the senses of a Frenchman.

"I found her admirable, and if I can I shall see her in another
part," he wrote. "She brings back to the dance that artistic nobility which has slipped away through all sorts of considerations that
have nothing to do with art. She is very beautiful, and is a perfect
mime."

The ballet itself, however, seemed ridiculously pretentious.
He described it as "a historical, patriotic, piedmontophil, germano-
phil, anticlerical, gallophobe ballet. The hero was a certain Pietro
Micca who, during the siege of Turin by the French in 1706, blew
himself up in a fort together with the attackers. This is the dénouement of the piece, and above the ruins of the fort there arises an
apotheosis of 'la Superga,' Victor Emmanuel and Free Italy." To a
Frenchman's eyes the ballet was full of absurdities. "Battles are
fought by dancing, conspirators perform *entrechats*, and actors
cross the stage with the gestures and *soubresauts* of madmen and
the maxillary grimaces of crocodiles.... Children are abducted,
mothers weep, heroines are armed with carbines, and the flag of
Savoy is paraded by girls in pink tights to the cheers of the public."

Rolland found it exceedingly difficult to reconcile this
strange production with his own conception of ballet. "Italian
ballet," he continued, "with its heavily rhythmed ensembles, its
army corps manoeuvres, and the arid military precision of its
great choreographic crowd scenes, seemed to me artistically puerile
and very barbarous when compared with French ballet. It is no
longer dance, but arms drill. In France taste would have to fall very
low to produce enthusiasm for such vulgar art, when we have

Virginia Zucchi as Paquita in *Paquita*
(Maryinsky Theatre, St. Petersburg,
1886). Photo: Bergamasco. *(Bakhrushin
Theatre Museum, Moscow)*

As Fenella in Auber's opera *Fenella (La
Muette de Portici)* (Maryinsky Theatre,
St. Petersburg, 1887). Photo: Bergamasco.
(Collection of Natalia Roslavleva)

Virginia Zucchi as Esmeralda in Act I of *Esmeralda* (Maryinsky Theatre, St. Petersburg, 1886). Photo: Bergamasco. *(Bakhrushin Theatre Museum, Moscow)*

In Act V of *Esmeralda* (Maryinsky Theatre, St. Petersburg, 1886). Photo: Bergamasco. *(Museo alla Scala, Milan)*

Virginia Zucchi as the leading Grace in the Bayreuth production of *Tannhäuser* in 1891. *(Museo alla Scala, Milan)*

The Venusberg scene in the Bayreuth production of *Tannhäuser* in 1891. Zucchi is the centre figure of the Three Graces at the left. Engraving after the painting by Friedrich Stahl. *(British Library, London)*

Virginia Zucchi's daughter, Marie, c. 1900.
(Courtesy of Mrs. Carla Hackett Quijano)

Virginia Zucchi (third from left) with her brother Vittorio, her granddaughter Virginia Merli and her daughter Marie, c. 1910. *(Courtesy of Mrs. Carla Hackett Quijano)*

Virginia Zucchi in 1917. Drawing by Leon Bakst. *(Ashmolean Museum, Oxford)*

The Jury at the Ballet Examinations at the Scala, Milan, 1928. In centre, Enrico Cecchetti; on his right, Virginia Zucchi; between them, Cia Fornaroli; third from right, Pierina Legnani; third from left, Vincenzo Celli. *(Dance Collection, New York Public Library)*

Virginia Zucchi in the garden of her villa at Cortemaggiore, 1928. A still taken from an amateur cine film. *(Dance Collection, New York Public Library)*

Virginia Zucchi and her niece Virginia Zucchi Hackett. *(Courtesy of Mrs. Carla Hackett Quijano)*

Four generations: Virginia Zucchi, her daughter Marie (right), her granddaughter Virginia Braun (foreground) and her great granddaughter Charlotte. *(Courtesy of Mrs. Carla Hackett Quijano)*

the tradition of an art that is very refined and perfect. So ... yesterday's performance would have given me little satisfaction if it had not been for Zucchi. But there was Zucchi. And she is a very great artist."[11]

It was her reputation as a mime that led, later that year, to the historic summons that reached her from Bayreuth, the small Bavarian town dedicated to the musical genius of Richard Wagner. Devoted Wagnerians, who despised ballet as a superficial entertainment having no place in the sublime works of their master, may well have been puzzled to learn that an Italian ballerina had been called to Bayreuth, but Frau Cosima Wagner, the composer's widow and spiritual heir, had not issued the invitation without long and careful thought.

The centre-piece of the Bayreuth Festival of 1891 was to be a new production of *Tannhäuser*, in which the Venusberg scene, added by Wagner for the Paris version of 1861, was to be given in a new staging. Lucien Petipa, who had originally arranged the choreography, had not been in sympathy with the music, and Frau Wagner was determined that the Venusberg scene should now be staged as her husband had conceived it, and in a way that would be both original and free from balletic condition. She therefore sought someone with a broader understanding of movement than a ballet-master in the traditional mould and decided that this quality was most likely to be possessed by an experienced mime. For a time she wavered in her choice between Virginia Zucchi, whose dramatic talent she greatly admired, and a mime from the Paris Opéra, and in her predicament she sought the advice of Gustavo Macchi. He left her in no doubt as to his opinion: Virginia Zucchi, he said, was the most original, the most intuitive and the least conventional person she could find.

So Julius Kniese, Frau Wagner's chorus director, accompanied by Macchi, went to Nice to put the proposition to Virginia and to explain discreetly that artists were invited, not engaged, to

take part in the Festival at Bayreuth and were rewarded not with a
fee but with a gift. They could not have received a warmer welcome.
No sooner did Macchi reveal the object of their visit than Virginia
clapped her hands in pleasure. To stage the Venusberg scene would
be a dream come true, she cried, a great honour! Kniese, whose
knowledge of Italian was slight, wanted to explain how Wagner had
conceived the idea and to talk about the practical problems involved.
But to his surprise Virginia knew the music well and then and there
sketched out the development of the scene as she envisaged it. On
the subject of remuneration, which Kniese found particularly em-
barrassing, she did not even wish to speak. "Signora Cosima," she
declared, "will do what she thinks best."

In August 1890 Virginia went to Bayreuth to meet Frau
Wagner. The two women took to one another at once. In a letter
to her son-in-law, Houston Chamberlain, Cosima told of the arrival
of Zucchi, "through whom we have come to experience that Italian
spontaneity which shines through her constant amiability. Whether
she will be equal to the enormous task which is to be given her
here. . . I do not know. I do know, however, that this human experience was heart-warming, and that this woman, with her sensi-
tiveness, her simplicity and her perseverance, has enriched our
little group. She has a magnificent head, and I have unconsciously
compared her to one of the Graces, even if she is no longer young,
not tall, and somewhat ample."[12]

The opera was not to be produced until the following summer, and Virginia's presence for rehearsals would not be required
for many months. She was therefore able to fulfil engagements at
the Teatro Dal Verma, Milan, and the Teatro Costanzi, Rome, in
the early summer of 1891. In Rome Marco Praga saw her in
Coppélia, and during an interval hurried to her dressing-room to
remind her of their plans for a recital.

"Signora Virginia, when is it to be?" he asked eagerly. "Do
you remember?"

"But it is just an obsession," she laughed, and she left him
to go on to the stage and see that everything was in order for the
next act, for she was impresario, star, manager and choreographer
all in one. Meanwhile Praga returned to his seat in the stalls, realising that his desire to hear her recite would never be fulfilled. He
was bitterly disappointed, for the idea had been with him for two
years, and he knew that the ballerina possessed that "natural gift
that is indispensable. . . for recitations, a voice both strong and caressing, warm of timbre, insinuating and most attractive. . . ."[13]

Virginia's mind was no doubt fixed on the task that awaited
her at Bayreuth. When she arrived there shortly afterwards she
found the town already stirring into life with the appearance of
singers, musicians, dancers and all the other theatrical personalities
who were to take part in the three operas that were to be produced
for the Festival: *Parsifal, Tristan und Isolde* and *Tannhäuser.* The
townfolk were busy, too, preparing for the flood of opera-lovers
who would be making the pilgrimage from all corners of the civi-
lised world to the shrine of the new German opera. Souvenirs
filled the shops, and busts of Wagner, portraits of his father-in-law
Liszt and photographs of the singers were everywhere to be seen.

The centre of activity was the Festival Theatre, the Festspielhaus, just outside the town. There Virginia found a spirit of
dedication, a striving for perfection that she had never experienced
before. Nothing was allowed to distract from the great work in
hand. Often the artists had no time to return to the town for lunch
after the morning's rehearsal and would cheerfully partake of a
good meal for the modest price of one mark in the large restaurant
adjacent to the theatre. There one might see Parsifal fraternising
with the Flower-maidens, celebrated musicians—among them
Engelbert Humperdinck and the young Richard Strauss, who were
répétiteurs that season—engaged in earnest talk, and Virginia
Zucchi relaxing after a morning's struggles with the thirty men and
thirty-four women who had been engaged, for the most part from

the Royal Opera in Berlin but with a sprinkling of Italians, for the
Venusberg scene. Then, as the clock struck the hour, it was time
to resume work, for with unfailing regularity, Frau Cosima's break,
drawn by two white horses, would at that very moment draw up
before the portico of the theatre to deposit the inspiring genius of
this busy world and her business manager, Adolf von Gross.

Under her supervision rehearsal followed rehearsal in clois-
ter-like seclusion, an old retainer of Frau Wagner's acting as watch-
dog to see that no stranger entered the theatre. As the Festival approached, however, the general rehearsals were opened to members
of the Wagner family and relatives of the artists, it being clearly
understood that this was done not as a favour to them but to enable the singers and musicians to experience the acoustics of a
filled auditorium.

At last the day arrived for the first performance: July 22nd,
1891. A long stream of carriages converged on the theatre, and the
audience took their seats in the auditorium under the watchful eye
of Cosima. Then, as always with absolute punctuality, the fanfare
sounded the motif of the Hunt to announce that *Tannhäuser* was
about to begin. The lights were extinguished, and only when complete silence reigned did the conductor raise his baton for the
overture.

The curtain rose for the first act on the Venusberg, the para-
disial abode of the goddess of love, where Tannhäuser has fallen under the sway of Venus but is now yearning to return to the earth.
Virginia's arrangement of this sensual scene, in which she herself
played one of the three Graces, was somewhat cramped by the
scenery which, as the correspondent of *The Times* observed, left
too little space for the dancers. "The complete realisation of the
composer's intentions with regard to the Bacchanalian orgy, which
plays so important a part in this scene," he continued, "is obviously
impossible, and it could not be more fully accomplished than was
done by the very excellent body of male and female dancers who
had been trained for the occasion by Signora Zucchi. . . . Unfortu-

nately the effect was much spoilt by the very clumsy and conventional dresses of the female members of the *corps de ballet*, in which
an unsuccessful attempt had been made to reproduce classical dra-
peries. On the other hand, the representatives of the Three Graces
were excellent, and the *tableaux* representing the Rape of Europa
and Leda and the swan were extremely beautiful in colour and
grouping."[14]

The excellent singing of Rosa Sucher as Venus added greatly
to the effect of the scene.

Virginia led a very simple existence in Bayreuth. The administration of the Festival had expected her to stay in the town's
leading hotel; but, typically, she preferred to be near the Italian
dancers she had brought with her and took a modest set of furnish-
ed rooms in a side-street near the Burgerreuthstrasse, the long
straight avenue that led to the Festspielhaus. It was here that the
music critic Aldo Noseda was directed to pay his respects and, to
his surprise, found her, with sleeves rolled up and arms covered with
flour, preparing *gnocchi*!

She accepted his invitation to supper on condition that they
eat during the interval between the second and third acts. "She
came," recalled Gustavo Macchi, who was included in the party,
"and sparkled with spontaneous humour and complete absence of
mannerisms, telling us everything that was going on backstage at
the theatre, and then ran off to see the last act."[15]

At Wahnfried, where the Wagner family lived, she became
everybody's favourite. Her artistic qualities were held in high respect by Cosima's circle, who fully appreciated the importance of
mime and expressive movement in theatrical production and were
anxious to experience her talent. Sometimes they were able to
persuade her to give them a private display, and she would then
good-humouredly drape herself in a table cloth and act the daggers
scene from *Brahma* while some eminent Wagnerian sat at the piano
and made what he could of the music of Dall'Argine.

Her visit to Bayreuth could not have been more successful, and it was followed very shortly afterwards, no doubt on the recommendation from Frau Cosima, by an invitation to stage the Venusberg scene for the new production of *Tannhäuser* at the Scala, Milan. Presented on December 26th, 1891, it had little success. For Virginia it was a very minor setback, and can have caused her little disappointment, for her thoughts were by then turned to the prospects that 1892 held in store for her.

It was both satisfying and reassuring to know that her services were still in demand. In the New Year of 1892 a return visit to St. Petersburg lay before her, with not only the prospect of renewing earlier triumphs, but the opportunity, which she may or may not have relished, of measuring herself against an actress with whom she had often been compared in their native Italy, Eleanora Duse. For a few weeks, at the Maly Theatre, her own ballet performances were to alternate with Duse's appearances in Italian drama—she as Padmana, Lise, Swanilda, Esmeralda and Sylvia; Duse as Nora, Cleopatra and the Lady of the Camellias—a juxtaposition of two great talents that must have prompted many fascinating comparisons of technique and style.

It was no secret that Virginia was now approaching the end of her career, and the Petersburg public, well-known for its fidelity towards its old favourites, filled the theatre on her opening night, January 27th, in a mood of sympathetic curiosity. Her old friend, Skalkovsky, had stayed away, not wishing to see her talent in decline, and his wisdom was all too soon apparent. For the years were now taking their toll: she was heavier both in her person and in her movements, and the magic of *Brahma* seemed to have slipped away. "The movements remain the same," wrote the critic of *Novosti*, "the eyes still flash, the enamoured girl still makes the menacing gesture that saves the life of her beloved, but a shadow had fallen on the brilliant palette of her acting, her eyes had lost their lustre. There was a sense of time passing. . . ."[16]

These melancholy reflections were soon put aside, and during the three weeks of her season the Maly Theatre was filled with an enthusiastic audience on every evening that she appeared. Something of her former brilliance might have dimmed, but in the mime scenes and the interpretative passages of her ballets she was still sublime. *Brahma* was followed by *La Fille mal gardée,* in which her Lise seemed as delightfully youthful as ever, even if she had to replace her famous leap in the *pas de deux* with a less exciting finish. She made a single appearance in the operetta, *Le Voyage dans la lune*, evoking memories of her first Russian summer, nearly seven years before. And she added a new role, Sylvia in Delibes' ballet of that name, which she learnt specially for the benefit performance of her partner, Giorgio Saracco.

At the end of February, when her contract had been fulfilled, Virginia left St. Petersburg, lying immaculate beneath its wintry blanket of snow, to seek the balmy warmth of the Mediterranean. Russia, which had given her unparalleled triumphs and to whose ballet tradition she had brought lasting enrichment, would not see her again.

Meanwhile, after his two seasons at Nice, Virginia's good friend, Raoul Gunsbourg, had developed a strong affection for the Riviera; and the artistic leanings of Princess Alice, the young American-born consort of the reigning Prince of Monaco, had drawn his attention to Monte Carlo as a suitable centre for his future activities. Being an employee of the Imperial court, he required permission to spend the winters outside Russia, and not only did he obtain this without difficulty on the grounds of frail health, but he extracted a recommendation from the Tsar for the post of Director of the Théâtre de Monte Carlo. With such backing his appointment was a foregone conclusion, and he took it up with the promise of strong support from the princess, who had ambitious plans to transform Monte Carlo, which for years had been dominated by the commercial fortunes of the Casino, into an international centre of the arts.

Gunsbourg thus arrived at a most propitious moment, to be immediately entranced by the jewel of a theatre that stood awaiting his guiding hand. Designed by Charles Garnier, the architect of the new Paris Opéra, in the florid Second Empire style, its sumptuous intimacy was the perfect setting for the grandiose plans he was laying to realise the vision of the princess. Now he needed a centre-piece for his first season that would irresistibly attract the social and musical worlds to Monte Carlo, and with characteristic temerity he offered what would be the first theatrical presentation of Ber-lioz's *La Damnation de Faust.*

Berlioz had not composed this work as a conventional opera, and for many years its very construction had inhibited impresarios from staging it in theatrical form. It had, in fact, become popular in Paris in the eighteen-seventies as a concert work. In later years musicologists were to allege that Gunsbourg's adaptation was not the scrupulous attempt to realise the composer's original intentions that he claimed it to be, but it was received very seriously at the time.

In adapting the libretto for the stage Gunsbourg had to de-cide how to present the symphonic passages of the score. His solu-tion was to accompany them with mimed action, and to give some of these scenes the required effect a powerful dramatic mime was essential. The invitation which he sent to Virginia Zucchi was not, therefore, a gesture to help an old friend who was approaching the end of her career, but a plea to the only artist who could realise the scenes that were taking shape in his imagination.

She joined him in Monte Carlo early in 1893. The rehears-als proceeded smoothly, and on February 18th the production was presented before a select audience. Prince Albert and Princess Alice presided in the gold and crimson state box, the Grand Duke Peter of Russia and many other royal princes were present, most of the leading music and theatre critics seemed to have made the

journey from Paris, and among the foreign visitors was Virginia's
friend, Alexandre Pleshcheyev, the Russian dance critic and historian. At the end of the evening praises were heard on all sides.
As a theatrical work the production had made a strong impression:
it held together dramatically, and the elements of dream and reality were interwoven with great skill.

Virginia played the image of Marguerite in the two dream
scenes. In Faust's Dream she first appeared as Marguerite dancing
among gnomes and sylphs and was then transformed into the spirit
of seduction, bending voluptuously over the sleeping figure of
Faust, caressing him and ravishing his senses. Later in the work
came the scene of Marguerite's Dream. Faust has concealed himself
in Marguerite's room, while Marguerite falls into an uneasy sleep.
To the Minuet of the Will-o'-the-Wisps, a sinister scene takes shape
in which Marguerite sees herself engaged in a bitter struggle with
Mephisto. Black-clad will-o'-the-wisps dance bizarrely around their
evil master. The figure of Marguerite tries desperately to escape,
only to be caught again each time she breaks free. She seeks comfort in prayer, but Mephisto's power is too strong, and she finally
succumbs. The terrible nightmare fades, and Marguerite awakes to
find herself in the arms of Faust.

So lavish was the praise of the local critic for Virginia's
miming that a reader who disapproved of dancers on principle
wrote an angry letter to the editor. The critic rose chivalrously to
her defence. "La Zucchi," he pointed out, "is an adorable actress
and an artist who is perhaps unique in her field, at least at the
present time. And you do not find Zucchis like that by the dozen,
I can assure you!"[17]

In the early summer of 1893 Virginia accepted engagements in Rome and Ancona, and in June visited London to nego-
tiate an engagement for the forthcoming Drury Lane pantomine,
Robinson Crusoe. One may wonder whether she understood the
popular nature of an English Christmas pantomime, which must
have seemed a strange sequel to the operas of Bayreuth and Monte

Carlo. But perhaps the fee was needed now that her engagements were becoming less frequent. The lack of interest shown in her by the London press was an added disappointment. The competition of Little Tich and Marie Lloyd, popular stars of the music hall, proved too strong for Virginia, who appeared, virtually unnoticed, in two short ballets by John D'Auban—a "grand fish ballet," *Revels under the Sea,* with Luigi Albertieri and the *Danse des sauvages* in the Golden Reef scene.

After the nightly chores of a London pantomime, it must have been a welcome relief to return to Monte Carlo. For his second season there Gunsbourg's plans included two operas in which Zucchi was to be featured. The first was César Franck's *Hulda,* produced on March 4th, 1894, in which she played Winter in a ballet of the Coming of Spring, making her entrance on *pointe* in an effectively staged snowstorm and engaging in a struggle with another Italian ballerina, Antonietta Bella, who played Spring. The other novelty, which followed on March 30th, was Isidore de Lara's *Amy Robsart*, an operatic version of Walter Scott's *Kenilworth* that had been successfully performed at Covent Garden the previous summer. In this Virginia was the Lady of the Lake in the scene of a masque performed before Queen Elizabeth, in which she was borne over the water on a floating island drawn by seahorses and tritons—a graceful figure in azure silk, with her black hair falling loose about her shoulders, coming with her nymphs to kneel before the Queen in an exquisite gesture of homage.

Apart from her annual visit to Monte Carlo, her engagements were now becoming shorter and less frequent. In the summer of 1894 she returned to Bayreuth for a few performances of *Tannhäuser* and in September appeared briefly in Lucca, but for the most part it was a fallow year. This was not wholly unwelcome, for she needed to conserve her strength for the arduous schedule that Gunsbourg was planning for her third season at Monte Carlo.

These plans included not only appearances in operas, but also a series of ballet performances at the Palais de Beaux Arts.

Here, from early in December 1894, she gave what were familiarly
known as her "five o'clocks" once or twice a week, presenting
miniature productions of *La Fille mal gardée, Esmeralda* and *Catarina.* Here, too, on February 23rd, 1895, she appeared in a new
pantomime by Léon Sarty called *La Pavane,* with a score by André
Pollonnais. In this innocent little piece she took the part of a high-
born girl with whom a Pierrot falls in love. In a moment of jealousy
he enlists in the army, but all ends happily when he returns, a
slightly wounded hero. In addition to these afternoon performances Virginia took part in two of the new opera productions at
the theatre, *La Gioconda* and *Armide,* but the responsibility for
the outstanding dance event of the season rested on other shoulders. The indefatigable Gunsbourg had succeeded in bringing to
Monte Carlo a group of dancers from the Russian Imperial Theatres who, led by Kshesinskaya, Preobrazhenskaya, Kyaksht and
Bekefy, created a sensation with a programme of classical and
character dances. Apart from individual visits by Russian dancers,
it was Western Europe's first experience of Russian ballet, and a
foretaste of the splendours that Diaghilev was to reveal fifteen
years later.

Now, with her career drawing to a close and thoughts of
new triumphs put aside, Virginia was to be granted the fulfilment
of a long-held ambition. For all her eminence, she had never, in
her heyday, set foot on the stage of the Paris Opéra, and that an
invitation should now come to her when her powers as a dancer
were on the wane was the Parisians' loss, not hers. For it was pri-
marily as a choreographer that she was engaged, on the insistance
of Cosima Wagner, to produce the Venusberg scene for a new production of *Tannhäuser.* To her added satisfaction, though, she was
also to take the part of one of the Three Graces as she had done in
Bayreuth, thus achieving, at last, the honour, greatly coveted by
all ballerinas, of appearing on the Opéra stage.

When this new production was first shown to the public on
May 13th, 1895, a few members of the audience could remember
the disastrous production of 1861 when the Jockey Club clique

had noisily vented their ire because the ballet had been inserted in the first act. Since then the attitude to Wagner had changed, and Virginia's arrangement of the Venusberg scene—hallowed by being the only authorised version—was received with all due respect. The movements of the dancers had been designed with a freedom from classical convention to which the Paris audience was unaccustomed, and while perceptive critics such as Alfred Bruneau recognised the original plastic quality of the choreography, others were perplexed by what seemed an absence of form. Maurice Ordonneau, for example, recalled that Lucien Petipa, the choreographer of the 1861 production, "had known how to bring order out of chaos."[18]

Virginia had not found it at all easy to produce this scene with the dancers of the Opéra, as Alfred Ernst, another critic, realised. "The bacchanale of the first act," he wrote, "is much too cold. It was mimed without passion, ardour or excitement by a group that was not large enough and whose routine style Mlle. Zucchi's efforts were unable to overcome. The celebrated Italian dancer tried in vain to obtain the violence, the fury, the frantic gyration of movement that Wagner's scenario and music demands. At Bayreuth Mlle. Zucchi had been guided by the personality of Frau Wagner that effectively impressed itself on everyone, down to the least important supernumerary."[19]

The most vivid description of the scene, as it was presented in Paris, came from the pen of Richard O'Monroy. "Groups of bacchantes invade the stage with head-dresses of vine leaves and tunics trimmed with fur. They are followed by fauns, and soon the dancing takes on a wilder character: the crotales, cymbals and tambourines sound as the bacchantes shake their beribboned thyrses. Then, at a sign from Venus, the cupids nestling in the trees loose their arrows at the dancers. Overcome by a sudden languor, the bacchantes and the fauns retire, and the Graces, portrayed by Mmes. Zucchi, Robin and Carré in pink peplum, return hand in hand to announce to Venus that calm has been restored." There followed a

series of *tableaux* at the back of the stage. "Europa passes on her
bull, and then a swan advances friskily on Leda, who is lying on a
bank. She stretches out her arms and—But then a cloud descends
from the flies and conceals everything from view. A pity! The old
abonnés were preparing themselves for a spectacle reserved for the
gods."[20]

Virginia spent the following winter in Monte Carlo, but in
contrast to her activity during the previous season, her stage appearances in the early weeks of 1896 were very infrequent. Apart from
a few performances of *La Damnation de Faust*, she was seen only
in a minor role in a pantomime with songs, *Mirka l'enchanteresse*,
that had been written for Adelina Patti. It now required a much
greater effort to appear before the public, but the lure of the footlights was still strong enough to tempt her back when an offer came
her way. At the end of 1896 she danced the pavane in Massenet's
Manon at the Dal Verme. Two years later, on August 20th, 1898,
she made a very belated first appearance at the Teatro Municipale
in Cortemaggiore. It was a performance in aid of charity, and she
brought her sister and some supporting dancers from Milan at her
own expense to give some scenes from *Brahma*. Only a worthy
cause could now lure her on to the stage, and her final appearance
as a dancer took place at the Dal Verme on November 16th, 1898,
when she played an important part in a gala organised for Marenco,
the composer of *Excelsior* and *Sieba*. She could not have chosen
two more fitting scenes to give a last glimpse of her versatile talent
than the doll scene from *Coppélia* and the harrowing finale of *Esmeralda*. For several months afterwards her name continued to be
featured in the list of dancers free to accept engagements that was
published in the *Gazzetta Teatrale Italiana*, but after April 1899 it
appeared no more. At the age of fifty it was time to retire.

However, she was still to make one more public appearance,
but not as a dancer. A year later a subscription was launched to
erect a monument in memory of Felice Cavallotti, a popular jour-

nalist who had been killed in a duel, and her friend, Gualtiero Solari, came to ask for her support. She willingly gave it, but in a way he had not anticipated. She proposed to give a recital, if he would accompany her. He could not refuse, and on September 21st, 1899, the two of them appeared at the Municipale in Cortemaggiore in a light comedy by Breccia, *Acqua o Carbone*. As they waited in the wings to make their entrance, she confessed that she had never felt more nervous in her life and alarmed him by taking a step back as if she were considering whether to go on at all. But a few minutes later she was on the stage in full control of herself. Recalling that evening many years later, Solari wrote: "She recited marvellously, as if she had done it all her life. . . . That minor work by Breccia was transformed, by her interpretation alone, into a masterpiece. She was restrained and elegant in her delivery, assured and refined in her gestures, natural in the tears which the tale of her sorrows required, and controlled in her animation when her whole being was filled with joy. A great actress would have recited no better, nor with more variety of expression, than she who was speaking on the stage for the first time. I no longer remember how many calls there were when I followed her before the curtain, but I must confess that the public's applause meant less to me than the unforgettable moment in the piece when Virginia Zucchi, as her part required, threw her lovely arms around my neck and kissed me. . . sincerely."[21]

The Years of Retirement

It is the dancer's lot, if she does not devote herself to teaching, to enter into a long period of retirement after her performing days are over, and almost inevitably to see her reputation dwindle. Younger celebrities appear to turn the heads of the public, golden memories fade, and audiences grow up for whom the dancers of the past are at most little more than names. All this lay in store for Virginia Zucchi when she put aside her costumes, ballet slippers and make-up box for the last time. In her case the process was even accelerated because she had not retired at the peak of her fame, but had reduced her exposure to the public gradually over a period of years—and indeed, as she herself must have admitted, beyond the moment when it would have been wisest to retire. Another contributory factor to the obscurity that clouded her career was the advent, little more than ten years after her retirement, of the Diaghilev Ballet. Its impact on the artistic and intellectual world of the West proved so shattering that the years before 1909 took on the appearance of a dark age, and with very few exceptions the dancers of the previous decades were forgotten. So it was that, in the new perspective that dance history assumed, Virginia, who in her day had been compared with the greatest actresses of the stage, was to receive much less attention than was her due.

This turn of events caused her little heartache or surprise, however, for in her own prime she had seen how dancers of earlier generations had been cast aside, and, taking a broader view, she must have derived satisfaction from the great renaissance of the art of ballet that Diaghilev stimulated. She had known the Imperial

ballet perhaps more intimately than anyone else in the West; she
had indentified herself with it and could share the Russians' pride
in their triumph; and she must have sensed that her own inspiration
had played no small part in enriching the tradition on which the
Diaghilev Ballet's achievement was founded.

As for herself, she had consciously sought tranquillity when
she retired from her career as a performer. Of course she could not
renounce her former vocation completely, but she maintained her
interest in the dance discreetly and away from the limelight. It was
the School of Ballet of the Scala that provided the link, and she
continued to attend the annual examinations as she had done for
some years before her retirement, concerning herself with the progress of some of the more promising students. In 1891 she had noticed the sixteen-year-old Carlotta Zambelli, who not only possessed a wonderfully pure style but was a natural comedienne. The girl
was giving such a comical performance of a mime scene from some
old ballet that Virginia found herself laughing until the tears rolled
down her cheeks. From that moment the two became firm friends,
and Virginia proudly followed the career of her "Zambellina", who
went on to become, for many years, the star ballerina of the Paris
Opéra.

Virginia never wanted for friends. Her natural warmth, her
down-to-earth simplicity and her jovial sense of humour endeared
her at once to everyone she met. Apparently she never married, but
this was not to say that she was not capable of strong passions. She
had indeed had her share of love affairs, but she was discreet
enough to ensure that what the public knew about them came not
from common gossip, but from confessions she deliberately let slip
in interviews with journalists, with no doubt a calculating eye to
their publicity value. The most serious of these affairs of the heart
seems never to have been publicly known. This was the association
with Adolphe Jourdan, the father of Marie. Marie grew to be a
ravishing beauty and inherited her mother's passionate nature. At

the age of sixteen she announced that she would not return to the convent where she was being educated. There was a violent scene which culminated in Marie's being given the choice between returning to the convent or marrying. She decided on the latter course and married a Signor Merli, by whom she had two daughters, Luisa, who died at the age of twelve, and Virginia. Living in Paris, Marie was able to pursue her artistic interests. She was a very gifted painter and knew many of the leading artists of Paris, including the venerable Paul Leroy, who may have been her teacher.

Marie's first marriage was not happy, and she left her husband and went to live with her mother in Paris. There she met Dr. Gaston Lacaze, who lived in Neuilly-sur-Seine and owned a large property, Blacieux, near Andance in the department of Ardèche. Dr. Lacaze was a small, friendly man with a white goatee and twinkling eyes, and he loved her dearly. Being much older than she, he worried greatly lest he die leaving her unprovided for. They went through a form of civil marriage in 1930, but it was not until after Signor Merli's death in 1942 that they were able to have a religious ceremony. Dr. Lacaze died in 1952, and the Château of Blacieux passed to Marie. The property was remembered by her young cousins as a sort of fairy-land, where they frolicked in the great woods and picked mushrooms in the golden summers of their childhood.

Shortly after the First World War Marie's daughter Virginia married a wealthy restaurateur, Albert Braun. It was a happy marriage, and in her old age Virginia Zucchi was to have the satisfaction of being photographed with her daughter, her granddaughter and, in her arms, her infant great-granddaughter—a group of four generations.

Virginia's sister Costantina had died in 1901 at the age of fifty. She, too, had been a dancer, but her career had been a modest one. In 1879–80 she achieved the ambition of many dancers by securing an engagement in Paris, but it was only on the very minor

stage of the Skating-Rink in the Rue Blanche, where she danced in
some early ballets by Mariquita. With the passing of her youth she
played mime roles, and in the year of her death her name was still
appearing in the *Gazzetta Teatrale Italiana* in the list of artists seeking engagements.

Of her two brothers, the elder, Achille, seems to have died
young. Vittorio, however, who had accompanied Virginia on
her travels as her secretary, remained a special favourite in spite of
his many faults. Indeed, so extreme was her attachment for him
that his son-in-law was led to wonder if he might not really be her
son. He was an incorrigible ne'er-do-well of irresistible charm, but
his talents—he was fluent in several languages—had been very useful
to his sister. He knew he would always be forgiven by her in the
end, even though he almost impoverished her with his gambling
debts and high living. In about 1895, after some exceptionally scan-
dalous incident, he was given a one-way ticket to America and settled in Albany, N.Y., where he met and married Louisa Schiutto,
who came from an immigrant family from Genoa.

Virginia disapproved of this marriage most strongly and,
when Vittorio returned to Italy in 1901 with his wife and two
baby daughters, she refused to have anything to do with her sister-
in-law and would never stay under the same roof with her, although
she continued to provide financial support for the family. A third
daughter, Natalina, was born not long before Vittorio contracted
tuberculosis following an attack of pneumonia. He died in 1913
and was buried in the family grave at Cortemaggiore, where his
remains now lie with those of his sisters. As for poor Louisa, she
was to be excluded from the family even in death, for she died in
1957 and was buried in Bennington, Vermont, a whole continent
away from Cortemaggiore.

Virginia had very definite plans for her two elder nieces,
which she set about fulfilling with little regard for the wishes of
their mother. She had not the slightest scruple about separating her
brother's family: she established her sister-in-law and the youngest

child in an apartment in Milan and took the other two, Virginia
and Maria, under her own wing to enter them in the School of
Ballet at La Scala. She imposed a strict discipline, but saw that they
were well provided for. There was, of course, no help forthcoming
from their parents, but Marie would send parcels of exquisite cast-
off clothing from Paris that were always opened with great excitement. Little Virginia was exceptionally promising as a dancer, and
her aunt built up great hopes for her and was soon announcing
proudly that she was to be her artistic heir. For most of the year
the child lived with her in her apartment in Milan, being looked after by a devoted old servant called Emilia.

Even her holidays were regulated by a strict routine. She
spent the summer months alone with her aunt either at the Villa
Zucchi in Cortemaggiore or at the Villa Olga in Alassio, which was
rented for the season, and was made to practise hour after hour,
every day. From time to time her aunt encouraged her by promising to stage *Coppélia* or *Fenella* for her when she was ready.

Shortly before the outbreak of the First World War she began to dance at the Scala under the name that her aunt had made
famous round the world. In 1917 she was prima ballerina at the
Teatro Colón in Buenos Aires, and she seemed on the threshold of
a successful career when she married the American tenor, Charles
Hackett, and retired to raise a family. "Zia Virginia" was deeply
wounded by what she took to be a betrayal, and her niece never
really felt she was forgiven.

The other niece, Maria, was less talented, and her aunt
quickly lost interest in her and thereafter ignored her completely.
During the short time that she danced professionally she never
attained the rank of soloist, and she, too, left the stage to marry.
The youngest of the three sisters, Natalina, never became a dancer
and settled in the United States.

When her two nieces had gone their separate ways, Virginia
spent less time in Milan and the apartment was empty for much of
the time. The solitude then became too much for the faithful

Emilia, who one day tried to end her life by throwing herself out of the window. Shortly afterwards Virginia gave up the apartment.

Despite the losses she had suffered as an impresario and the depredations caused by her brother, her theatrical career had left her comfortably provided for. Apart from her property at Cortemaggiore she owned a villa at Nervi and some vineyards. Most of her time in retirement she spent in Paris and on the Riviera, usually staying in hotels and going frequently to the opera and the theatre. A favourite resort was Monte Carlo, where she habitually spent her winters. One attraction was the company of her old friend, Raoul Gunsbourg, who was still directing the Opera there, and another was the Casino. She enjoyed watching the gamblers, although she herself rarely placed a stake and then only on the red or black.

In her later years her capital was severely eroded by losses resulting from speculative investments, in particularly a large holding of Russian railway shares which became worthless after the Revolution. Sadly, her income became insufficient for her needs, and her family noticed that the large cabinet in her Milan apartment containing many of the precious gifts she had received during her career gradually became emptier as, one by one, these treasures found their way to the sale-room.

In the autumn of her life she often visited Léon Bakst, who in 1917 drew her portrait, emphasising the imbalance of her features and catching the slight cast in her eye that added such a piquant touch to her appearance. On another occasion when she visited Bakst, some years after the War, the critic Valerian Svetlov was present, too, and inevitably the conversation turned to St. Petersburg and the Russian ballet and to the many friends she had made there, Skalkovsky in particular. Svetlov reminded her of the ballet shoe she had given to Skalkovsky and which had eventually found its way into his own collection. Then they spoke of Skalkovsky's famous phrase about the poetry of her back. It was an emotional moment.

"The old lady trembled with agitation at all these old recollections," wrote Svetlov. "She was at that time a thin, small woman with hair that was getting very gray, but dishevelled and wild as in her youth, earning for her the nickname of 'Rumple Peter,'* but her eyes sparkled brightly at the recollections of her triumphs and filled with moisture when Bakst spoke of the terrible misfortune that had overtaken Russia."[1]

To many who saw her in the 1920s it seemed she had discovered the secret of life, for she never lost her happy temperament and those little quirks that her friends found so endearing. Her obsession with odd superstitions was as strong as ever and, if her eyes caught sight of a horseshoe or even a piece of old iron in the street, she would still quickly pick it up and stuff it into her handbag for luck. It was impossible to think of her as an old lady. To Julia Sedova, who saw her giving a class in Monte Carlo after the War, she "seemed no more than sixty. Her figure was rather slim, and had retained its regularity of lines."[2] A few family snapshots have preserved the appearance of the divine Virginia in retirement, and a more vivid record still is a moving picture taken of her in the garden of her villa at Cortemaggiore in 1928.[3] The masculine turn of her features that had been noticeable even in her prime had become accentuated, but her erect figure and her ease of movement seemed unaffected by the passing of the years.

Of all the changes that had taken place in the development of ballet since her youth, one in particular must have caused her great sadness—the rapid decline, almost to extinction, of the Milanese school in which she had been trained. In the early nineteen-hundreds the ballet at the Scala became virtually dormant, and in 1917 the School of Ballet was closed. It was reopened in 1921, but the choice of a Russian, Olga Preobrazhenskaya, as its first director was sadly significant. For a few years the School struggled on under

---

*A more accurate translation of the nickname she was given in Russia, *Strepka-Rastrepka,* would be "Shock-headed Steve."

a succession of directors. Then, in 1925, hopes of a regeneration were raised when Toscanini, who had become the theatre's Artistic Director, invited Cecchetti to take over the School of Ballet, and for several years Virginia took her place on the Jury at the annual examinations. Often sitting with her on these occasions was Pierina Legnani, another celebrated representative of the Milanese school, but now retaining only the vestiges of her former charms. She had turned into a dowdy old lady, inseparable from an untidy umbrella with a red parrot's head handle that all too unfortunately matched the colour of her nose.

It was at the 1927 examinations that Anna Pavlova met these two ballerinas of a generation before her own. Legnani, whom she had seen dance at the Maryinsky, she only "recognised with some difficulty," but Virginia Zucchi, who till then had only been a great name from the past, fascinated her. She seemed "so active, elegant and upright that she did not at all give the impression of an old woman."[4] After making some rapid calculations, she realised, incredulously, that Zucchi must be nearly twenty years older than Legnani. With some hesitation she asked Cecchetti if he knew her age and was quite taken aback when he gave her a precise answer in Virginia's hearing.

That autumn Madame Cecchetti died and, when Virginia met the Maestro next at the following year's examinations, she could hardly recognise her one-time partner in the pathetic, wasted old man who greeted her. At the end, when the photographer began to arrange the group, Cecchetti was reluctant to be included, pointing out the consequences of there being thirteen in the picture. Superstitious though she was, this did not seem to trouble Virginia in the least.

"Oh, for Heaven's sake, don't worry," she said. "The oldest among us will be the next to die, and that's me."

So Cecchetti took his place in the group, looking sadly at the camera as if he knew that his end was near. A few months later he collapsed while taking a class and died the following day.

After his passing Virginia was seen no more at the Scala. The spirit that had kept her youthful was now beginning to falter, and the end came quietly and peacefully, as she would have wished. In the autumn of 1930 she took to her bed in her room at the Hôtel d'Angleterre in Nice,* and there, shortly before midnight on October 9th, her body, once so expressively pliant, became still and the fire in her beautiful eyes, which had burned so stirringly in the days of her glory, flickered and died away.

There remained only the final solemnity. Her body was taken to Cortemaggiore, and there the family gathered to pay their last respects to the formidable personality who had dominated their lives. Among them was Vittorio's widow who had been so mercilessly ignored by the deceased in her lifetime and yet had been irresistibly drawn to participate in the obsequies. But she was not permitted to share the family grief: no one spoke to her, she was not invited back to the villa and at the end of the day she returned sadly to Milan by the train. She had brought with her her granddaughter Carla Hackett, who was thirteen and had been allowed out of school to attend the funeral. For a child it was a frightening experience, for which no one had thought to prepare her. Seemingly for hours she stood shivering in the dim, dank church by the side of the black-draped catafalque. Then, at last, she took her place in the procession to the cemetery and walked behind the glass-sided hearse with its black horses and black trappings and feathers, while a great brass band played terrifying funeral music. She had nightmares for months afterwards and, as she grew older, the experience acquired in her memory an almost surrealist flavour. Perhaps, with her child's imagination, she had caught the awesome significance of the occasion, marking as it did not merely the end of an individual existence, but the disappearance of an artistic genius that had enhanced an age.

*The Hôtel d'Angleterre was then owned by Charles Braun, whose son had married Marie's daughter Virginia. It was also in Nice that Marie died, in 1959.

With the committal of her mortal remains to the earth of her homeland, the life of Virginia Zucchi had completed its full circle. Her passing was almost as private as her coming into the world more than eighty years before. This was as it should have been, for, while the echoes of her ovations had long since died away, the contribution she had made to the art of the dance was woven imperishably in its tradition. As emerges with crystal clarity from the memories of those who came under her influence, she was beyond all doubt one of the greatest inspiratory ballerinas of all time. It was not out of idle flattery that she was vaunted in her heyday, and is now remembered by history, as the Divine Virginia.

Notes

A Miracle Indeed! (pages 1-8)

1. Haskell, *Ballet Panorama*, p. 69.
2. Giarelli, *La Scena Illustrata*, 15 March 1888.
3. Haskell, *Diaghileff*, p. 132.
4. Romanovsky-Krassinsky, p. 26.
5. Legat, p. 5.
6. Svetlov, *Archives Internationales de la Danse*, 15 Oct. 1934.
7. Svetlov, *Dancing Times*, Dec. 1930.
8. Haskell, *Diaghileff*, pp. 131-132.
9. Benois, *Zhizn Khudozhnika*, v. II, p. 51 (trans. Moura Budberg).

A Local Reputation in the Making (pages 9-20)

1. *Gazzetta dei Teatri*, 22 April 1886.
2. *Il Mondo Artistico*, 22 Aug. 1877.
3. *La Fama*, 7 Nov. 1865.
4. *Gazzetta dei Teatri*, 4 Nov. 1865.
5. Quoted in *La Fama*, 30 Oct. 1866.
6. *La Fama*, 28 March 1867.
7. *La Fama*, 16 June 1868.
8. *La Fama*, 2 Nov. 1869.
9. Wilczek, p. 185.
10. Stoullig Press Cuttings, Rj 4193, I, pp. 457, 476-478.

Spreading Fame (pages 21-37)

1. Stoullig Press Cuttings, Rj 4193, I, p. 456.
2. *La Fama*, 22 Sept. 1874.
3. Ferrarini, p. 94.
4. *Gazzetta Musicale di Milano*, 2 Jan. 1876.
5. *La Fama*, 22 Feb. 1876.
6. *Gazzetta Musicale di Milano*. 2 Jan. 1876.

7. Racster, pp. 72-73.
8. *Berlinische Zeitung*, 16 May 1876.
9. Stoullig Press Cuttings, Rj 4193, I, p. 457.
10. *Pungolo*, quoted in *Gazzetta dei Teatri*, 9 Aug. 1877.
11. *Illustrated Sporting and Dramatic News*, 15 June 1878.
12. Quoted in *Gazzetta dei Teatri*, 6 Jan. 1881.
13. *Gazzetta dei Teatri*, 14 April 1881.
14. *Gazzetta dei Teatri*, 7 April 1881.
15. *Il Caricaturista*, 22 Jan. 1882.
16. *Asmodeo*, 14 Feb. 1882.
17. *Gazzetta dei Teatri*, 23 Feb. 1883.
18. *Il Caricaturista*, 4 March 1883.
19. *Le Figaro*, 23 Nov. 1883.

The Paris Eden (pages 38-54)

1. *Le Clairon*, 23 Nov. 1883.
2. Un Pompier, pp. 15-16.
3. *Spirit of the Times*, 29 Dec. 1883.
4. Stoullig Press Cuttings, Rj 4193, I, p. 477.
5. *Evènement*, 24 Nov. 1883.
6. *Le Gaulois*, 23 Nov. 1883.
7. Stoullig Press Cuttings, Rj 4193, I, p. 480.
8. Stoullig Press Cuttings, Rj 4193, I, p. 477.
9. Stoullig Press Cuttings, Rj 4193, I, p. 477.
10. Stoullig Press Cuttings, Rj 4193, I, p. 480.
11. Stoullig Press Cuttings, Rj 4193, I, p. 480.
12. Champsaur, *Miss América*, pp. 48-50.
13. Champsaur, *L'Amant des danseuses*, pp. 13-15.
14. Champsaur, *L'Amant des danseuses*, pp. 24-26.
15. *Peterburgsky Listok*, 9/21 Oct. 1889.

Kin Grust (pages 55-73)

1. Skalkovsky, *Balet*, p. 144.
2. Skalkovsky, *B Teatralnom Mire*, p. 122.
3. *Vsemirnaya Illyustratsiya*, 1885, No. 863, p. 79.
4. Pleshcheyev, *Pod Seniyu Kulis*, p. 125.
5. *Novoye Vremya*, 8/20 June 1885.
6. *Peterburgskaya Gazeta*, 11/23 June 1885.

7. *Teatralny Mirok*, 15/27 June 1885.
8. Benois, *Reminiscences*, p. 76.
9. Skalkovsky, *B Teatralnom Mire*, pp. 113-115.
10. Skalkovsky, *B. Teatralnom Mire*, pp. xxvi-xxvii.
11. Khudekov, vol. IV, p. 21
12. *Novoye Vremya*, 11/23 July 1885.
13. *Novoye Vremya*, 11/23 July 1885.
14. Skalkovsky, *B Teatralnom Mire*, p. 127.
15. Skalkovsky, *B Teatralnom Mire*, p. 125.
16. Skalkovsky, *B Teatralnom Mire*, p. 127.
17. Benois, *Reminiscences*, pp. 78-80
18. Pleshcheyev, *Nash Balet*, p. 271, and *Chto Vspomnilos*, pp. 210-211.
19. *Journal de St. Petersburg*, 11/23 Aug. 1885.
20. S.A.Andreyevsky in *Novoye Vremya*, quoted by Pleshcheyev, *Nash Balet*, p. 282.
21. *Teatralny Mirok*, 17/29 Aug. 1885.
22. Kshesinski, book II, fol. 25-26.

The Imperial Stage: Aspiccia and Lise (pages 74-92)

1. Central State Historical Archives, Moscow, f. 497, op. 5, d. 3388.
2. Lunacharsky State Theatre Library, Leningrad.
3. Benois, *Reminiscences*, pp. 81-82.
4. Benois, *Reminiscences*, p. 83.
5. *Novoye Vremya*, 12/24 Nov. 1885.
6. *Novosti*, 13/25 Nov. 1885.
7. *Novoye Vremya*, 12/24 Nov. 1885.
8. *Sanktpeterburgskiye Vedomosti*, 10/22 Nov. 1885.
9. Khudekov, vol. III, pp. 352-353 and vol. IV, pp. 121-122.
10. Benois, *Reminiscences*, p. 85.
11. Benois, *Reminiscences*, p. 82.
12. Lieven, p. 58.
13. Benois, *Reminiscences*, pp. 83-84.
14. Racster, pp. 134-135.
15. *Teatralny Mirok*, 16/28 Nov. 1885.
16. Racster, pp. 59-60.
17. Pleshcheyev, *Nash Balet*, p. 274.
18. *Sanktpeterburgskiye Vedomosti*, No. 318, 1885.
19. *Souffleur*, 19/31 Dec. 1885.
20. Benois, *Reminiscences*, p. 89.
21. Averkiev, p. 36.
22. *Novosti*, 20 Dec. 1885/1 Jan. 1886.

23. *Novoye Vremya*, 17/29 Dec. 1885.
24. Benois, *Reminiscences*, p. 90.
25. Benois, *Reminiscences*, p. 92.
26. Benois, *Reminiscences*, p. 94.
27. Pleshcheyev, *Pod Seniyu Kulis*, p. 132.
28. *Teatralny Mirok*, No. 2, 1886.
29. Lunacharsky State Theatre Library, Leningrad.

"Esmeralda" at the Maryinsky (pages 93-108)

 1. Lieven, p. 61.
 2. *Teatralny Mirok*, Nos. 23/38 and 24/39, 1886.
 3. *Teatr i Zhizn*, 19/31 Oct. 1886.
 4. *Journal de St. Pétersbourg*, 21 Oct./2 Nov. 1886.
 5. *Teatr i Zhizn*, No. 150, 1886.
 6. *Novoye Vremya*, 4/16 Nov. 1886.
 7. *Teatr i Zhizn*, No. 202, 1886.
 8. *Novoye Vremya*, 19/31 Dec. 1886.
 9. *Novosti*, 19/31 Dec. 1886.
10. *Dnevnik Teatrala*, 15/27 Jan. 1889.
11. *Dnevnik Teatrala*, 15/27 Jan. 1889.
12. *Novoye Vremya*, 19/31 Dec. 1887.
13. *Dnevnik Teatrala*, 15/27 Jan. 1889.
14. *Dnevnik Teatrala*, 15/27 Jan. 1889.
15. Velizary, pp. 54-55.
16. Romanovsky-Krassinsky, pp. 26-27.
17. Drizen, p. 35.
18. Central State Historical Archives, Moscow, f. 497, op. 5, d. 3388.
19. *Journal de St. Pétersbourg*, 29 Jan./10 Feb. 1887.
20. *Syn Otechestva*, 21 Jan./2 Feb. 1887.
21. *Syn Otechestva*, 21 Jan./2 Feb. 1887.
22. *Syn Otechestva*, No. 28, 1887.

Farewell to the Imperial Stage (pages 109-120)

 1. *Kurier Codzienny*, 12 June 1887.
 2. *Kurier Warszawski*, 27 June 1887.
 3. *Journal de St. Pétersbourg*, 8/20 July 1887.
 4. *Journal de St. Pétersbourg*, 20 Nov./2 Dec. 1887.
 5. *Journal de St. Pétersbourg*, 20 Nov./2 Dec. 1887.
 6. Racster, p. 132.

7. *Journal de St. Pétersbourg*, 24 Nov./6 Dec. 1887.
8. Pleshcheyev, *Nash Balet*, p. 305.
9. Information supplied by Yuri Slonimsky, who had it from Alexandre Shiryaev, who was dancing at the Maryinsky Theatre during Zucchi's seasons there.
10. *Novosti*, 19/31 Jan. 1888.
11. *Novoye Vremya*, 19/31 Jan. 1888.
12. *Journal de St. Pétersbourg*, 19/31 Jan. 1888.
13. Skalkovsky, p. 167.
14. *Syn Otechestva*, 18/30 Jan. 1888.
15. *Syn Otechestva*, 5/17 March 1888.
16. *Birzhevie Vedomosti*, 11/23 March 1888.
17. *Birzhevie Vedomosti*, 14/26 March 1888.
18. Skalkovsky, p. 177.
19. *Gazzetta dei Teatri*, 13 Jan. 1887.
20. *Novosti*, 18 Feb./1 March 1888.
21. *Le Figaro*, 11 March 1888.
22. Pleshcheyev, *Pod Seniyu Kulis*, p. 132.

An Unproductive Interlude (pages 121-138)

1. Giuri memoirs.
2. Letter from Yuri Bakhrushin to Ivor Guest, 3 Dec. 1961.
3. Giuri memoirs.
4. *Teatr i Zhizn*, No. 126, 1888.
5. *Novosti*, 18/30 Aug. 1888.
6. *Birzhevie Vedomosti*, 4/16 Nov. 1888.
7. *Dnevnik Teatrala*, 15/27 Jan. 1889.
8. *Novosti*, 26 Nov./8 Dec. 1888.
9. *Teatr i Zhizn*, No. 211, 1888.
10. Stanislavsky, pp. 127-128 (Penguin ed.)
11. *Novosti*, 5/17 Feb. 1889.
12. Skalkovsky, p. 185.
13. *Le Gaulois*, 30 Jan. 1890.
14. *Novosti*, 13/25 May 1889.
15. *Journal de St. Pétersbourg*, 13/25 May 1889.
16. Repin and Stasov, p. 140.
17. *Journal de St. Pétersbourg*, 1/13 July 1889.
18. *Novoye Vremya*, 30 June/12 July 1889.
19. *Novosti*, 30 June/12 July 1889.

The Riviera and Bayreuth (pages 139-160)

1. *Gazzetta dei Teatri*, 22 April 1886.
2. *Gazzetta dei Teatri*, 31 Oct. 1889.
3. *Gazzetta dei Teatri*, 21 Nov. 1889.
4. Praga, *Scena-Sport*, 1 June 1891.
5. Gunsbourg, pp. 109-110.
6. *Le Petit Niçois*, 21 Jan. 1890.
7. *Le Temps*, 3 Feb. 1890.
8. Khudekov, vol. III, p. 353.
9. *Gazzetta dei Teatri*, 17 April 1890.
10. *Gazzetta dei Teatri*, 23 April 1891.
11. Rolland, pp. 252-254.
12. Cosima Wagner-Houston Chamberlain correspondence, p. 183. Letter dated 6 Aug. 1890.
13. Praga, *Scena-Sport*, 1 June 1891.
14. *The Times*, 29 July 1891.
15. *Giornale degli Artisti*, 18 Oct. 1930.
16. *Novosti*, 17/29 Jan. 1892.
17. *Les Rives d'Or*, 12 March 1893.
18. *Le Matin*, 14 May 1895.
19. *Revue Encyclopédique*, 1 June 1895.
20. *Gil Blas*, 13 May 1895.
21. Solari, *Giornale dell' Arte*, 23 Nov. 1930.

The Years of Retirement (pages 161-170)

1. Svetlov, *Dancing Times*, Dec. 1930.
2. Svetlov, *Dancing Times*, Dec. 1930
3. Now in the Dance Collection of the Museum of Performing Arts, New York.
4. Dandré, p. 18.

Bibliography

Alheim, P. d' *Sur les pointes* (Paris, 1897)

Benois, Alexandre *Reminiscences of the Russian Ballet* (London, 1941)

Bottura, G.C. *Storia del Teatro Comunale di Trieste* (Trieste, 1885)

Brunelli, Bruno *I Teatri di Padova* (Padua, 1921)

Capetti, Ugo "Stelle dietro le nubi : V. Virginia Zucchi" (*Gazzetta dei Teatri*, Milan, 22 April 1886)

Carozzi, Enrico *Annuario Teatrale Italiano per l'annata 1886* (Milan, 1886)

Champsaur, Félicien *L'Amant des danseuses* (Paris, 1888)

Champsaur, Félicien *Miss América* (Paris, 1885)

Dandré, Victor *Anna Pavlova in Art and Life* (London, 1932)

De Filippis, F. and Arnese, R. *Cronache del Teatro di S. Carlo* (Naples, 1961-63)

D'O[rmeville], C[arlo] "Virginia Zucchi" *(Gazzetta dei Teatri*, Milan, 8 December 1892)

Ferrarini, Mario *Parma Teatrale Ottocentesca* (Parma, 1946)

Gatti, Carlo *Il Teatro alla Scala* (Milan, 1965)

Giarelli, Francesco "La Baiadera della civiltà" *(La Scena Illustrata,* Florence & Rome, 15 March 1888)

Giarelli, Francesco *Vent'anni di Giornalismo* (Codogno, 1896)

Guest, Ivor *Carlotta Zambelli* (Paris, 1969)

Guest, Ivor *La Fille mal gardée* (London, 1960)

Gunsbourg, Raoul *Cent ans de souvenirs* (Monaco, 1959)

Haskell, Arnold L. *Balletomania* (London, 1934)

Haskell, Arnold L. *Ballet Panorama* (London, 1938)

Haskell, Arnold L. *Diaghileff* (London, 1935)

Incogliati, Matteo *Il Teatro Costanza* (Rome, 1907)

Lavignac, Albert *Le Voyage artistique à Bayreuth* (Paris, 1897)

Legat, Nicolas *Ballet Russe* (London, 1939)

Levitan, Joseph "Virginia Zucchi" *(Der Tanz,* Berlin, November 1930)

Lieven, Prince Peter   *The Birth of Ballets-Russes* (London, 1936)

Limouzin, Charles   *Almanach illustré de Monaco et de Monte Carlo, 1895* (Nice, 1894)

Millenkovich-Morold, Max   *Cosima Wagner* (Leipzig, 1934)

Monaldi, Gino   *Le Regine della Danza nel Secolo XIX* (Turin, 1910)

Morini, Ugo   *La R. Accademia degli Immobile e il suo teatro "La Pergola", 1649-1925* (Pisa, 1926)

Pallerotti, A.   *Spettacoli melodrammatici e coreografici rappresentati in Padova* (Padua, 1892)

Pompier, Un   *Un Coin de l'Eden* (Paris, 1886)

Praga, Marco   "Virginia Zucchi" *(Scena-Sport,* Florence, 1 June 1891)

Pretzsch, Paul (ed.)   *Cosima Wagner und Houston S. Chamberlain im Briefwechsel* (Leipzig, 1934)

Racster, Olga   *Master of the Russian Ballet* (London, 1922)

Rasi, Luigi   *La Caricatura e i Comici Italiani* (Florence, 1907)

Rollain, Romain   *Retour au Palais Farnèse* (Paris, 1956)

Romani, Luigi   *Teatro alla Scala* (Milan, 1862)

Romanovsky-Krassinsky, S.A.S. la Princesse   *Dancing in Petersburg-The Memoirs of Kschessinska* (London, 1960)

Roslavleva, Natalia   *Era of the Russian Ballet* (London, 1966)

Sacerdote, Giacomo   *Teatro Regio di Torino* (Turin, 1892)

Solari, Gualtiero   "Virginia Zucchi" *(Giornale dell'Arte,*   Milan, 23 November 1930)

Svetlov, Valerian   "Virginia Zucchi" *(Dancing Times,* London, December 1930)

Svetlov, Valerian   "Les Étoiles étrangères en Russie" *(Archives Internationales de la Danse,* Paris, 15 October 1934)

Travaglia, Silvio   *Riccardo Drigo, l'uomo e l'artista* (Padua, 1929)

Vallabone, G.B.   *Il Teatro Carlo Felice* (Genoa, 1928)

Works in Russian

Аверкиев, Д. В.   *Дневник писателя Д. В. А., 1885-1886.* (СПБ, 1887)

Балетоман [В. Скалковский]   *Балет, его история и место в ряду изящных искусств* (СПБ, 1882)

Бахрушин, Ю. А.   *История русского балета* (М, 1965)

Бенуа, А. *Жизнь художника* (Нью-Йорк, 1955)

Борисоглебский, М. *Материалы по истории русского балета* (Л, 1938-39)

Велизарий, М. И. *Путь провинциальной актрисы* (Л-М, 1938)

Всеволодский-Гернгросс, В. Н. *Краткий курс истории русского театра* (М, 1936)

Дризен, Н. В. *Сорок лет театра* (П, 1916)

Кашкин, Н. Д. *Воспоминания о П. И. Чайковском* (М, 1954)

Красовская, В. М. *Русский балетный театр второй половины XIX века* (Л, 1963)

Плещеев, А. А. *Наш балет, 1673-1899* (СПБ, 1899)

Плещеев, А. А. *Под сению кулис* (Париж, 1936)

Плещеев, А. А. *Что вспомнилось* (СПБ, 1914)

Репин, И. Е. и Стасов, В. В. *Переписка* (Л, 1949)

Скальковский, В. *В театральном мире* (СПБ, 1899)

Слонимский, Ю. Из воспоминании Риккардо Дриго (*Музыкальная жизнь*, № 23, М, 1973)

Слонимский, Ю. *Тщетная предосторожность* (Л, 1961)

Станиславский, К. *Моя жизнь в искусстве* (Л-М, 1931)

Столпянский, П. Летопись Петербургских Императорских театров, 1881/ 82 — 1885/86 (*Ежегодник Императорских Театров*, СПБ, 1912-14)

Худеков, С. *История танцев, тт. III и IV* (П, 1915, 1918)

Manuscripts

Джури, Аделина *Мемуары* (Центральная научная библиотека ВТО)

Кшесинский, И. *Мемуары* (ЦТМБ)

Newspapers and Periodicals

ITALY: Asmodeo, Corriere della Sera, La Fama, Gazzetta dei Teatri, Gazzetta Musicale di Milano, Gazzetta Teatrale Italiana, Il Mondo Artistica, Teatro Illustrato, Il Trovatore.

PARIS: Le Clairon, Evènement, L'Europe Artiste, Le Figaro, Le Gaulois, Gazette de France, Gil Blas, Le Temps.

NICE: Le Petit Niçois.

MONTO CARLO: Les Rives d'Or.

LONDON: Era, Illustrated London News, Illustrated Sporting and Dramatic News, The Times

BERLIN: Berlinische Zeitung, Neue Preussische Zeitung.

WARSAW: Kurier Codzienny, Kurier Warsawsky.

ST. PETERSBURG: Биржевые ведомости, Всемирная иллюстрация, Новое время, Новости, Нувеллист, Петербургская газета, Петербургский листок, Суфлер, Сын отечества, Театральный мирок, Journal de St. Pétersbourg.

MOSCOW: Артист, Будильник, Дневник театрала, Жизнь искусства, Новости сезона, Русские ведомости, Сезон, Театр и жизнь, Театр.

Index

181

about the author . . .

Ivor Guest was born in Chislehurst, Kent, England. He was educated at
Lancing College and the University of Cambridge, where he received an M.A.
degree in Law. After serving in the British Army during World War II, he
entered the legal profession as a Solicitor. Simultaneously, he began writing
on the history of ballet. Mr. Guest was a regular contributor to Richard
Buckle's *Ballet* magazine, and has published more than eighteen books on
dance. He organized the exhibition "Books on Ballet" for the National
Book League (1957-1958) and contributed to the creation of Sir Frederick
Ashton's *La Fille mal gardée* by discovering the early scores. Mr. Guest
joined the Executive Committee of the Royal Academy of Dancing in 1965,
and became Chairman in 1969. He is married to Ann Hutchinson, the
authority on dance notation.